Res Care of Children

Fergus Smith
B.Sc.(Hons), M.A., C.Q.S.W., D.M.S., Dip.M

CAe

Children Act Enterprises Ltd (CAE)
103 Mayfield Road
South Croydon
Surrey CR2 0BH

www.caeuk.org

© Fergus Smith 2005

British Library Cataloguing in Publication Data
A catalogue record for this book is available from the British Library

ISBN 978-1-899986-42-2

Designed and typeset by Andrew Haig & Associates
Printed in the UK by The Lavenham Press

All rights reserved. Except as permitted under the Copyright, Designs and Patents Act 1988, this publication may not be reproduced, stored in a retrieval system, or transmitted in any form or by any means, without the prior written permission of the publisher.

CAE is an independent organisation which publishes guides to family and criminal law and provides consultancy, research, training and independent investigation services to the public, private and voluntary sectors.

No part of this publication may be reproduced without the written consent of the author.

Contents

Introduction	1
Definitions	2
Routes into Residential Care	4
Local Authority General Duties Towards Looked After Children	7
Arranging Placements – Obligations of Responsible Authority	10
Limiting/Refusing Contact for Child in Care	20
Independent Visitors	23
Advocacy Service	25
Reviews	26
Looking After Children: Good Parenting, Good Outcomes (LAC System)	32

Children's Homes Regulations

General (1–5)	34
Registered Persons (6–10)	39
Welfare of Children (11– 24)	42
Staffing (25–27)	56
Records (28–30)	60
Premises (31–32)	67
Management of Home (33–36)	71
Miscellaneous (37–43)	76

Registration Regulations

Applications	82
Register & Certificate	84
Conditions & Reports & Cancellation of Registration	85

Fees & Frequency of Inspections Regulations

Registration Fees	88
Variation Fees	89
Annual Fees	90
Frequency of Inspection	91

National Minimum Standards: Children's Homes

Introduction	94

Planning for Care

Written Statement of Home's Purpose (1)	95
Placement Plans (2)	97
Reviews (3)	99
Contact (4)	101
Moving In & Leaving the Home (5)	102
Preparation for Leaving Care (6)	104
Support to Individual Children (7)	107

Quality of Care

Consultation (8)	110
Privacy & Confidentiality (9)	112
Provision & Preparation of Meals (10)	115
Personal Appearance, Clothing, Requisites & Pocket Money (11)	117
Good Health & Well Being (12)	119
Treatment & Administration of Medicines within the Home (13)	122
Education (14)	125
Leisure & Activities (15)	127

Complaints and Protection

Complaints & Representation (16)	130
Child Protection Procedures & Training (17)	133

Countering Bullying (18)	137
Absence of Child without Authority (19)	139
Notification of Significant Events (20)	142

Care and Control
Relationship with Children (21)	144
Behaviour Management (22)	146

Environment
Location, Design & Size of the Home (23)	150
Accommodation (24)	152
Bathroom & Washing Facilities (25)	154
Health, Safety & Security (26)	158

Staffing
Vetting of Staff & Visitors (27)	160
Staff Support (28)	164
Overall Competence of Staff (29)	167
Sufficient Numbers of Staff (30)	170
Training and Development (31)	173

Management and Administration
Monitoring by Person Carry On the Home (32)	175
Monitoring of Operation of the Home (33)	176
Business Management (34)	178
Children's Individual Case Files (35)	180

Specialist Provision
Secure Accommodation & Refuges (36)	181

Appendices
1: Policy Issues for Inclusion in Staff Guidance	184
2: Programmes of Training for Staff	187
3: Source Documents	189
4. CAE Publications	190

Abbreviations

ACA 2002 = Adoption and Children Act 2002

CA 1989 = Children Act 1989

CAFCASS = Children & Families Courts Advisory & Support Service

CRB = Criminal Records Bureau

CSA 2000 = Care Standards Act 2000

CSCI = Commission for Social Care Inspection

CYPA 1969 = Children and Young Persons' Act 1969

PACE 1984 = Police and Criminal Evidence Act 1984

POCA 1999 = Protection of Children Act 1999

Introduction

- This guide is designed for use by all those in England who provide or work in children's homes (comparable regulations and standards apply to boarding, and residential special schools).

- The guide is intended to facilitate understanding of obligations and expectations of the Care Standards Act 2000 (CSA 2000), Children Act 1989 (CA 1989), other relevant regulations and national minimum standards.

- The Commission for Social Care Inspection (CSCI) (with effect from April 2007, Ofsted) will assess, on the basis of the mandatory Children's Homes Regulations 2001 - SI 2001 3967 and achievement of the national minimum standards (issued by the Secretary of State under s.23 (1) CSA 2000), whether a children's home should be registered.

- CSCI may issue a written warning to a service provider which is failing to achieve a required standard. It also has the power to take enforcement action by cancelling registration or initiating a criminal prosecution.

- If CSCI makes any decision about registration, cancellation, variation or imposition of conditions, it must take into account the national minimum standards and any other factors considered reasonable and relevant. The DfES is currently consulting about the possibility of amending regulations and standards relevant to Children's Homes.

Definitions (in alphabetical order)

Child

- A person aged less than 18 years old.

Children's Home [s.1 CSA 2000]

- An establishment is a children's home if it provides care and accommodation wholly or mainly for children.

- An establishment is not a children's home:
    - Merely because a child is cared for and accommodated there by a parent/relative or foster carer
    - If it is a health service or independent hospital or clinic, residential family centre, school (but see below) or is of a description excepted by regulation

- A school **is** a children's home if at that time accommodation is provided for children at the school and either:
    - In each of the previous 2 years, accommodation was provided for children at the school or under arrangements made by the proprietor for more than 295 days or
    - It is intended to provide such accommodation for children

Looked After [s.22 CA 1989]

- A child who is 'looked after by a local authority may be 'accommodated', 'in care' or 'remanded/detained.

- Accommodation is a voluntary arrangement, the local authority does not gain parental responsibility and no notice is required for removal of the child.

- In care means that a court has made a child subject of a Care Order which gives the local authority parental responsibility and (some) authority to limit the parents' exercise of their continuing parental responsibility.

- The local authority has specific authority to detain those who fall into the third category (though with the exception of Emergency Protection Orders, the local authority does not gain parental responsibility), and it may do so as a result of:

    - Remand by a court following criminal charges
    - Detention following arrest by police
    - An Emergency Protection Order or a Child Assessment Order
    - A 'criminal' Supervision Order with a residence requirement

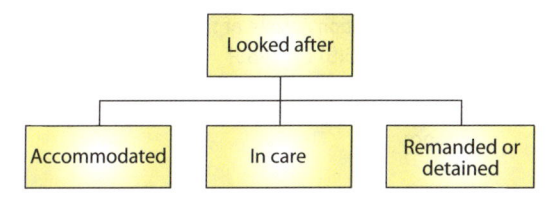

```
                    Looked after
                         |
        ┌────────────────┼────────────────┐
   Accommodated       In care      Remanded or
                                    detained
```

Routes into Residential Care

Accommodating a Child [s.20 CA 1989]

- One of the family support services the local authority must provide is that of 'accommodating' (in family or residential settings) anyone under 18 'in need' who requires it as a result of:

  - There being no person with parental responsibility for her/him
  - S/he being lost or having been abandoned or
  - The person who has been caring for her/him being prevented temporarily or permanently (for whatever reason) from providing suitable care/accommodation

- This service is a completely voluntary arrangement and the local authority does not gain parental responsibility.

- A person with parental responsibility has the right to remove a child from such an arrangement [s.20(8) CA 1989] but:

  - A holder of a sole Residence Order could authorise the retention of a child in accommodation in spite of the parent's wishes to remove [s.20(9) CA 1989]
  - A young person of 16 or 17 could overrule the parent's wishes to remove her/him [s.20(11) CA 1989]

- Anyone who does not have parental responsibility for a child but does have actual care of her/him may do what is reasonable in the circumstances to safeguard and promote the child's welfare [s.3 (5) CA 1989].

- If 'significant harm' seems likely, emergency protection measures could be used.

Accommodating a 16 or 17 Year Old [s.20 (3) CA 1989]

- A local authority must provide accommodation to a young person in the above age group if:
    - S/he is 'in need' and her/his welfare would otherwise be 'seriously prejudiced'

Accommodating a Young Person Aged 16–20 Years Old [s.20 (5) CA 1989]

- A local authority may provide accommodation in any Community Home which accepts 16+ year olds if it considers it would safeguard or promote the young person's welfare.

Other Obligations To Accommodate [s.21 (1), (2) CA 1989]

- When asked, the local authority must accommodate those:
    - Removed from home on an Emergency Protection Order, Child Assessment Order or an Interim Care Order

- In Police Protection
- Remanded by a court
- Detained under Police & Criminal Evidence Act 1984
- On a Supervision Order with residence requirements (Children & Young Persons Act 1969 [s.12AA]

Local Authority General Duties towards 'Looked After' Children [ss.22, 23, 24 & Sch.2 CA 1989]

- The local authority must safeguard and promote the child's welfare and make reasonable efforts to allow her/him access to ordinary services as though still at home.

- The local authority must endeavour, unless not reasonably practical or consistent with her/his welfare, to promote contact between the child and

  - Parents, and others with parental responsibility
  - Relatives, friends or persons connected with her/him

- The local authority must take reasonable steps to keep parents and those with parental responsibility informed of the child's location.

- Before making any decision, the local authority must ascertain the wishes and feelings of the:

  - Child
  - Parent/s and any others who have parental responsibility, and relevant others

- The local authority must give due consideration to these views (having regard in case of the child to her/his level of understanding) religion, racial origin, cultural and linguistic background.

NB. A local authority may act contrary to the above in order to protect the public from serious injury.

- So far as is practical and consistent with welfare, the local authority must place the child with:
  - Parents
  - Someone who has parental responsibility
  - (For a child in care), any previous Residence Order holder
  - Relatives or friends or
  - Other person connected with her/him

- If a child has to be placed with strangers, the local authority must ensure the placement is near home and with any siblings.

- The local authority is obliged to prepare the child for leaving looked after status.

- The local authority must also take reasonable steps to:
  - Reduce criminal/civil proceedings which might lead to Care or Supervision Orders
  - Avoid the use of secure accommodation
  - Encourage children not to commit crime

Additional Duties towards a Child with a Disability

- Work with children who have a disability should be based on the principles:
  - They are children first and their disability is a

secondary, albeit significant issue
- Promotion of access to the same range of services for all

■ Local authorities:
- Must, so far as is practical, when they provide accommodation for a disabled child, ensure that the accommodation is not unsuitable for her/needs. [s.23(8) CA 1989]
- Must maintain, for forward planning purposes, a register of children who have a disability [Sch. 2 para.2 CA 1989]
- May, assess a child's needs for the purpose of the Children Act at the same time as any assessment under certain other Acts, e.g. Education Act 1996. Sch.2 para. 3 CA 1989]
- Must provide services for children who have a disability which are designed to minimise the effects of the disability and give them the opportunity to lead as normal lives as possible [Sch.2 para. 6 CA 1989]

NB. The rights of disabled children to consent to or refuse assessment/treatment or access their records is limited only by the general conditions regarding sufficient understanding which apply to other children under the Children Act 1989 [see companion personal guide to 'Child Protection' for further details].

Arranging Placements – Obligations of Responsible Authority

Arrangements for Placements of Children (General) Regulations 1991 as amended

- The above regulations describe the obligations of what is termed the 'responsible authority' when it makes a placement of a child.

- For a child looked after and placed by a local authority (in any placement including voluntary or private home) the local authority is the responsible authority.

- For a child accommodated and placed by a voluntary organisation (in whatever setting) the responsible authority is that voluntary organisation.

- For the very few neither looked after by a local authority nor accommodated by a voluntary organisation the private home which accommodates them becomes the responsible authority.

NB. The Arrangement Regulations do not apply to placements of a child (other than by a local authority or voluntary organisation) in independent schools which are considered to be children's homes, nor to non-maintained special schools not maintained by a local education authority or out of public funds. [Reg.3 The Children (Homes, Arrangements for Placements, Reviews and Representations) (Miscellaneous Amendments) Regulations 1993].

Placement Plan [Reg.3 Arrangement Regulations]

- Before a placement is made the responsible authority must, so far as is reasonably practical construct a written immediate and long term plan.
- Where impractical to do so before the placement begins it must be done as soon as reasonably practical following the placement.
- The arrangements must normally be made with a person with parental responsibility or if there is no such person, with the current caregiver. For an individual of 16 or 17 accommodated despite parental objection, the arrangements should be with her/him.

Notification of Arrangements [Reg.5 Arrangement Regulations]

- So far as is reasonably practical, the responsible authority must provide advance written notification of the arrangements to place a child to:
    - Anyone whose wishes and feelings were sought prior to the placement by the local authority, voluntary organisation or private home provider respectively [ss.22(4), 61(2), 64(2) CA 1989]
    - The primary care trust (PCT) (or if there is no PCT, the health authority for the area in which the child is living) and if it is different for the area in which s/he is to be placed
    - Local education authority for the area in which the child is living and in which s/he is to be placed

Arranging Placements

- The child's registered medical practitioner and, where applicable, any registered medical practitioner with whom the child is to be registered following the placement
- Any person who was caring for the child immediately before the placement
- Any person in whose favour there is a Contact Order (unless the child is 'in care')
- Any person who has contact with the child as a result of a court order under s.34 CA 1989 (contact with a child in care by parents etc)
- The 'area authority' i.e. the local authority for the area in which the child is placed when this is not her/his own local authority

■ Where impractical to provide advance notice it must be given as soon as possible after the placement begins.

■ The responsible authority must also send with this notification:

- As much of the placement plan as it believes will not prejudice the welfare of the child to those whose wishes/feelings were sought prior to placement
- Such details as it believes they need to know to the other agencies/individuals cited above

Contents of Plan [Reg. 4 & Schs. 1, 2 & 3 Arrangement Regulations]

General Matters

- The aim of the placement and time scale should be contained in a written plan as should:
  - The proposed support for it
  - A contingency position if the desired plan fails
  - All identifiable needs including those arising from race, language, religion and culture
  - Agreed allocation of tasks
  - Dates of reviews

- Where the local authority is the responsible authority it must consider whether it needs to seek a change in the child's legal status e.g. should an application be made to discharge a Care Order

- Arrangements for contact and any need to change them and the duty to promote contact (consistent with welfare) with family and relevant others must also be considered.

- Previous arrangements, any need for change and current immediate and long term proposals must be examined.

- In the case of a local authority, the possible need for an independent visitor considered.

- Whether arrangements are needed for child's departure from looked after or accommodated status.

- Whether plans are needed to find a permanent substitute family.

Health Matters

- Child's state of health and health history.

  NB. Records should include developmental history, illnesses, e.g. operations, immunisations, allergies, medication, appointments with G.P. etc. but not the antibody status of those known to be HIV positive which should be held on a 'need to know' basis only.

- Effect of health/health history on her/his development.

- Current arrangements for medical/dental care and treatment, health and dental surveillance identifying any required changes.

- Any need for immunisations or sight or hearing screening.

Educational Matters

- Child's educational history and need to achieve continuity.

- Identification of educational needs and plan to meet them.

- Possible need to carry out assessment under Education Act 1996 and meet any special educational needs thereby identified.

Arranging Placements

Matters to Be Included For Those Not In Care

- Address and type of accommodation to be provided and name of any person who will be responsible there, for the child on behalf of the responsible authority.

- Details of any services to be provided for child.

- Respective responsibilities of child, any parent of her/his, any non-parent who has parental responsibility detailing what delegation of day to day care those with parental responsibility have agreed with the responsible authority.

- Arrangements for involving above persons in decision making.

  NB. Local authorities are obliged by s.20(6) & s.22(3)-(5) CA 1989 to involve children in decision making before accommodating them and to ascertain and give due consideration to the wishes and feelings of them and parents while looking after them.

  Voluntary organisations & private homes have comparable duties in respect of those for whom they are caring [s.61 (1) & (2), & s.64 (1) & (2) CA 1989 respectively].

- Arrangements for contact and any changes in these including (where appropriate) reasons why contact would not reasonably practical or would be inconsistent with the child's welfare, between child and:

- Parents
- Anyone else who has parental responsibility for them
- Friends, relatives or persons connected with them

NB. Voluntary organisations & private homes must, unless it is not reasonably practical or consistent with welfare of the child try to promote contact between her/him and the above persons.

■ Where appropriate, confirmation that s.20 (11) CA 1989 (accommodation of a young person of 16 or over despite parental opposition) applies.

■ The expected duration of the arrangements and steps which should be taken to end it, e.g. how to achieve rehabilitation with the person with whom child was living previously or with another suitable person.

Health Requirements [Reg. 7 Arrangements Regulations]

■ Residents of homes are especially vulnerable to a lack of continuity of health care.

■ Unless completed within the 3 months prior to placement, a responsible authority must:

- Ensure arrangements are made for assessment of child's health (may include a physical examination) by a doctor
- Ask the doctor to provide a written assessment of the child health and any needs as listed in Sch. 2 Arrangement Regulations

Arranging Placements

- When it is not reasonably practical to make these arrangements before a placement they must be made as soon as practical after it begins.
- A child of sufficient understanding may refuse such an assessment [Reg.7 (4) Children Act (Miscellaneous Amendments) (England) Regulations 2002].

  NB. If the resident's stay is likely to be short or the home is in her/his own locality, it is usually preferable to use the resident's G.P. and s/he should be given the opportunity of using a doctor of the same sex.

- A responsible authority must ensure that each child is provided during her/his placement with:
  - Health care services including medical and dental care and treatment and
  - Advice and guidance on health, personal care and health promotion issues appropriate to her/his needs

Establishment, Retention & Confidentiality of Records [Regs. 8 & 9 Arrangement Regulations]

- Each responsible authority must maintain written case records for every child it places.
- These records must include:
  - A copy of the 'placement plan'
  - Any written report about the child's welfare it possesses
  - A copy of any records/documents connected with a case review

- - Details of contact arrangements, any contact or other court orders
  - Details of any arrangements for another person to act on behalf of the local authority or organisation which placed the child

- Records (originals, paper copies or other e.g. computer) must be kept by the responsible authority until the child person is 75 or (should s/he die before 18 years of age) for 15 years after her/his death.

- Records must be stored securely and their contents treated as confidential unless:
  - A law allows access to them, e.g. an officer of Children & Families Courts Advisory and Support Service (CAFCASS) – children's guardian etc, has a right of access to all records concerning a child belonging to or held by a local authority [s.42 CA 1989 as amended] and to those maintained by those who run voluntary and private homes [Reg. 11 Arrangements Regulations]
  - A court order obliges access to be given

Register of Placements [Reg. 10 Arrangements Regulations]

- A local authority is obliged to maintain a register of those placed in its area (by it and other responsible authorities) as well as those it places outside the area.

- A voluntary organisation and anyone carrying on a private home must also keep a register of those placed by them.

- Registers must contain considerable detail prescribed in paras. 3 & 4 of Regulation 10 about the child and the placement.

- Details on the register must be retained until the child is 23 or if s/he dies before then, for 5 years after death.

Short -Term Placements [Reg.13 Arrangement Regulations as amended by Reg.3 The Children (Short-Term Placements) (Miscellaneous Amendments Regulations) 1995

- A series of placements in the same place may be treated as a single placement if:
    - All placements occur within a period of a year or less
    - No single placement lasts more than 4 weeks and
    - The total duration of the placements does not exceed 120 days

Limiting/Refusing Contact for Child In Care [s.34 CA 1989 & Contact with Children Regs. 1991]

Contact Plan [s.34 (2), (3) CA 1989]

- Courts must consider the proposed contact arrangements between child and parents and other involved relatives before making a Care Order. [s.34 (11) CA 1989.]

- Directions as to contact may be given on the court's initiative or as a response to an application made by :

  - The local authority
  - The child
  - Parents/guardian
  - A person who either held a Residence Order or had care of the child by virtue of an order made under the High Court's inherent jurisdiction, immediately before the Care Order was made
  - Any other person with court's permission

NB. Contact may be by means of letters, telephone, photographs or any other method as well as visits.

Local authorities are empowered to help with the cost of visiting residents where there would otherwise be undue hardship. [Sch.2 para.16 CA 1989].

Limiting/Refusing Contact for Child in Care

Planned Refusal of Contact [s.34 (4) CA 1989]

- The court may, in response to an application by the local authority or child make an order which allows the authority to refuse contact between the child and any of the persons listed in the contact plan section above.

- Orders under s.34 can be made at the same time the Care Order is made or later, and may be varied or discharged on the application of the local authority, child or the person named in the order.

Emergency Refusal of Contact [s.34 (6) CA 1989]

- A local authority can refuse to allow the normal 'reasonable contact', or that directed by the court if:
  - It is satisfied that it is necessary to do so to safeguard and promote the child's welfare and
  - Refusal is urgent and does not last more than 7 days

- When a local authority has decided to refuse contact in this way, it must immediately provide written notification to the following persons:
  - The child (if of sufficient understanding)
  - Her/his parents or guardian
  - Anyone who immediately before the Care Order was made, held a Residence Order or had care by virtue of an order made under the High Court's inherent jurisdiction and
  - Anyone else whose wishes and feelings it considers relevant

- Notification must contain as much of the following as the local authority believes these persons need to know:
    - The decision and the date it was made
    - Reasons for the decision, and, if applicable
    - How long it will last (max. 7 days)
    - How to challenge the decision

Departure from Terms of Court Order about Contact under s.34 [Reg. 3 Contact Regulations]

- A local authority can depart from the terms of an order made by the court if the person named in the order agrees and:
    - Where the child is of sufficient understanding, s/he also agrees
    - Written notification has been sent within 7 days

Other Variations or Suspension of Contact [Reg. 4 Contact Regulations]

- Where a local authority varies or suspends contact arrangements other than those made as a result of a court order under s.34 in order to allow a person contact with a child in care, it must also provide written notification.

    NB. The obligations as to content and distribution of notifications about departure from terms of court orders or other variations or suspension of contact arrangements are identical to those described in the section on emergency refusal of contact above.

Independent Visitors [Sch. 2 Para.17 CA 1989] & Definition of Independent Visitors (Children) Regulations 1991]

- The local authority must appoint an independent visitor when a child is being looked after by a local authority and:
    - The contact between her/him and a parent or other person who has parental responsibility has been infrequent or
    - S/he has not visited, been visited or lived with any of these people during the last 12 months and
    - It would be in the best interest of the child
- The role of the independent visitor is to visit, advise and befriend the child.

    NB. An independent visitor must be acceptable to a resident (who, if of sufficient understanding, has a right to refuse a proposed person) and if s/he has any special needs the visitor should have or be helped to develop relevant skills, e.g. Makaton.

    An independent visitor is entitled to reclaim reasonable expenses from the local authority.

- A person may only be regarded as independent of the local authority if s/he is unconnected with the local authority i.e. is not a councillor, officer or their spouse.

- In the case of a child in accommodation other than that provided by the local authority, the visitor can only be regarded as independent if s/he is not a member, patron, trustee or employee (paid or not) of that organisation, nor a spouse of any of these persons.

DH guidance suggests that 'spouse' could justifiably include a person in a stable cohabitation.

Advocacy Service [s.26A CA introduced by s.119 ACA 2002]

- Every local authority is obliged to make arrangements for the provision of assistance (including representation) to children and care leavers who wish to make a complaint under the provisions of the Children Act 1989.
- The Advocacy Services and Representations Procedure (Children) (Amendment) Regulations 2004 (as well as amending the existing regulations to ensure that an advocate is involved at **all** stages of the complaints process) specify that:
    - Persons who may **not** act as the advocate e.g. manager of the service about which complaint made
    - The complainant must be informed of the advocacy service and helped to access it
    - The local authority must monitor compliance with these regulations

Reviews [s.26 CA 1989 & Review of Children's Cases Regulations 1991]

Review of Children's Cases Regulations 1991]

- For a child looked after by a local authority, the responsible authority for ensuring compliance with the above regulations is that local authority.

- For a child not looked after by a local authority but provided with accommodation by a voluntary organisation, the responsible authority is that organisation.

- The person carrying on the home is the responsible authority for a child not placed by a local authority or voluntary organisation but accommodated in a private home.

  NB. The Review Regulations do not apply to a child who is being provided with accommodation (otherwise than on behalf of a local authority or voluntary organisation) in an independent school considered to be a children's home under s.63(6) CA 1989 or in a special school not maintained by a local education authority or out of public funds.

Frequency of Reviews [Reg.2 Review Regulations 1991]

- Each case must be reviewed at the following intervals:

- Within 4 weeks of a child becoming looked after or accommodated
- Not more then 3 months after the first review
- Not more than 6 months after the previous review

NB. These are minimum intervals and additional reviews may be convened in response to particular circumstances or at request of parent or resident.

Health Reviews [Reg. 6 Review Regulations 1991]

- The responsible authority must make arrangements for those who continue to be looked after/accommodated by it to receive a health assessment (which may include a physical examination) and for a written report addressing matters listed in Sch.2 to be prepared at intervals of no more than:

  - 6 months for those under 5 years of age and
  - 12 months for those over 5

- The health assessment may be conducted by a registered medical practitioner or a registered nurse or midwife acting under her/his supervision and should inform the review of the plan for the future health of the child prepared under the Arrangement Regulations.

- A child of sufficient understanding may refuse to consent to such an assessment.

Procedures for Review, Consultation, Participation & Notification [Regs. 4, 7 & 10 Review Regulations 1991]

- Each responsible authority should have written procedures for the conduct of reviews which should be made known to service users.

- Before conducting any review the responsible authority must, unless it is not reasonably practical, seek and take into account the views of:

  - The child
  - Her/his parents
  - Any person other than a parent who has parental responsibility and
  - Anyone else whose views the local authority considers could be relevant to the review, e.g. foster carers, residential staff, teachers, health visitor, G.P.

- The above people must also, as far as is practical be:

  - Involved in the review, attending for as much of it as is thought appropriate
  - Notified of the results of the review and of any decisions taken as a result of it

  NB. The venue for a review should be chosen, in consultation with parent/s and residents to encourage participation. Financial or practical support to attend should, where necessary, be provided.

Any decision to exclude a parent or resident from the review should be recorded and placed on file.

- The responsible authority must ensure that information obtained as a result of a review, minutes of meetings and decisions made are recorded in writing.

Issues for Consideration before or at Reviews [Regs.4, 5, 6 & Sch.1, 2 & 3 Review Regulations 1991]

- So far as is practical the responsible authority must consider:

  - Before reviews, making necessary preparations, e.g. initiating meetings of relevant staff of the responsible authority/other relevant persons and providing relevant information to potential participants
  - At reviews, the current arrangements, any relevant changes in the child's circumstances, and any consequent need to alter the immediate or long term plan (including the steps which will be necessary to implement such change)
  - Names and addresses of people whose views should be taken into account
  - Explaining to the child any steps s/he may take under the Children Act 1989, e.g. where appropriate the right to apply with the court's leave for a s.8 order, if in Care, to apply for a discharge of the Care Order and the existence of the complaints procedure

- For those in care whether an application should be made to discharge the Care Order
- Where the local authority is the responsible authority, whether it should seek a change in the child's legal status and/or appoint an independent visitor
- Contact arrangements and any need for change in relation to family and friends
- Educational needs, progress and development as well as any special arrangements which have been or need to be made, e.g. assessments under Education Act 1996
- Individual and as far as is practicable, family health history, current physical, emotional and mental health and their effects on development
- Existing arrangements for medical/dental treatment and surveillance, possible need for change including preventive measures such as vaccination/screening for vision or hearing and need for advice on health, personal care and health promotion issues
- Necessary arrangements for leaving care system
- Any need to plan for a permanent substitute family

NB. The possibility of child needing to bring someone to support her/him should be considered as should any need to organise separate attendance by parents.

Placement for Short Periods [Reg. 11 Review Regulations 1991 as amended by Reg.5 Children (Short-Term Placements) (Miscellaneous Amendments) Regulations 1995]

- A series of placements with the same caregiver or in the same home may be regarded as a single one for the purpose of these regulations if:

    - All the periods are contained within 12 months
    - No single period exceeds 4 weeks and
    - Total duration of the periods does not exceed 120 days

    NB. In such short breaks/shared care arrangements, the time limit within which the first review must be held is 3 months from the beginning of the first of the short periods.

Looking After Children: Good Parenting, Good Outcomes [LAC System]

- Effective use of the LAC system, including proper completion of Planning and Review Forms and Assessment and Action (A&A) Records will ensure all the above obligations with respect to arrangements, placements and reviews are met.

- Carers should:
  - Encourage the child to share in the completion of the Records and in contributing to the Planning and Review Forms
  - If necessary, remind the social worker / case manager of the importance of use of the LAC system

NB. The LAC system is scheduled to be replaced with the Integrated Children's System (ICS) in 2007.

Children's Homes Regulations

General [Regs. 1–5 Children's Homes Regulations 2001]

- The registered person in relation to a children's home means any person who is the registered provider or registered manager of that home.

- The registered manager in relation to a children's home means a person who is registered under Part II of the CSA 2000 as the manager of that home.

- The registered provider in relation to a children's home means a person who is registered under Part II of the CSA 2000 as the person carrying on that home.

Excepted Establishments [Reg. 3 Children's Homes Regulations 2001]

- The following are excepted from being a children's home:
  - Any institution within the further education sector as defined by s.91(3) Further and Higher Education Act 1992
  - Any establishment providing accommodation for children for fewer than 28 days in any 12 months in relation to any 1 child for purposes of a holiday or recreational, sporting, cultural or educational activity
  - Any premises at which a person provides day care within the meaning of Part XA CA 1989 for

fewer than 28 days in any 12 month period in relation to any 1 child
- Any establishment providing accommodation for children aged 16 or over to enable them to undergo training or apprenticeship, for a holiday or for recreational, cultural or educational purposes
- Any approved bail or probation hostel
- Any institution provided for young offenders under or by virtue of s.43(1) Prison Act 1952

*NB. The exceptions in the last 5 categories above do **not** apply if the children accommodated are wholly or mainly 'of a description falling within s.3(2) CSA 2000' i.e. they have physical or mental illnesses, are disabled or have been dependent on drugs or alcohol.*

For purposes of calculating the 28 days specified in category 3 above, no account is taken of any period of 24 hours during which at least 9 are spent by a child in the care of her/his parent or relative and day care is not being provided for the child during that time.

Statement of Purpose and Children's Guide [Regs. 4, 5 & Sch. 1 Children's Homes Regulations 2001]

- The registered person must compile a 'statement of purpose' which includes:

  - The overall aims of the home and objectives to be attained with respect to residents
  - A statement of facilities and services to be provided

General

- Name and address of registered provider and registered manager if applicable
- Relevant qualifications and experience of persons working at the home, and if workers all of same sex, a description of the means whereby the home will promote appropriate role models of both sexes
- Arrangements for supervision, training and development of employees
- Organisational structure of the home
- Particulars about age range, sex, numbers of residents, whether it is intended to accommodate disabled children, those with special needs or nay other special characteristics and the range of other needs the home is intended to meet
- Admission criteria, including home's policy and procedures (where relevant) for emergency admissions
- For homes with capacity for over 6 residents, a description of the positive outcomes intended and the strategy for counteracting any adverse effects on children arising from the home's size
- A description of the home's underlying ethos and philosophy and where this is based upon any theoretical or therapeutic model, a description of that model
- Arrangements made to protect and promote the health of children
- Arrangements for promotion of the education of residents including the facilities for private study

- Arrangements to promote children's participation in recreational, sporting and cultural activities
- Arrangements made for consultation with residents about the operation of the home
- Arrangements made for control, restraint and discipline of children
- Arrangements made for child protection and to counter bullying
- Procedure for dealing with any unauthorised absence of a child
- A description of any electronic or mechanical means of surveillance which may be used
- Fire precautions and associated emergency procedures
- Arrangements for contact between child and parents, relatives and friends
- Arrangements for dealing with complaints
- Arrangements for dealing with reviews of placements
- Type of accommodation, including sleeping accommodation, provided and where applicable how children are to be grouped and in what circumstances they are to share rooms
- Details of any specific therapeutic techniques used and arrangements for their supervision
- A description of the homes policy in relation to anti-discriminatory practice as respects children and children's rights

■ The registered person must provide a copy of the statement of purpose to CSCI and make a copy of it available upon request for its inspection, by:

- Any person who works at the home
- Any actual or potential resident
- The parent of any resident
- The placing authority
- (In the case of a 'qualifying school') the Secretary of State and Her Majesty's Inspector of Schools in England

■ The registered person must also produce a 'children's guide' to the home which includes:

- A summary of the home's statement of purpose
- A summary of the Reg. 24 complaints procedure
- Address and telephone number of CSCI

■ The children's guide must be produced in a form appropriate to the age, understanding and communication needs of residents.

■ Copies of the children's guide must be given, on admission, to all residents and a copy supplied to CSCI.

■ The registered person must keep under review and where appropriate, revise the statement of purpose and children's guide, notify the CSCI within 28 days of any such revision and ensure that residents receive the updated children's guide.

Registered Persons [Regs. 6–10 Children's Homes Regulations 2001]

Fitness of Registered Provider [Reg. 6 Children's Homes Regulations 2001]

- A person must not carry on a children's home unless s/he is fit to do so.

- A person is not fit to carry on a home trading either as an individual, a partner or an organisation unless all specified requirements are satisfied.

- The requirements are that:
  - Each individual is of integrity and good character
  - S/he is physically and mentally fit to carry on a home
  - Full and satisfactory information is available about the person as detailed in paras. 1–6 of Sch. 2 Children's Homes Regulations 2001 (prior to the implementation of ss.113 & 115 Police Act 1997) and paras. 1 and 3–7 (after their implementation)

- A person is not allowed to carry on a children's home if s/he is an un-discharged bankrupt or has made an arrangement with creditors in respect of which s/he has not been discharged.

Appointment of Manager [Reg. 7 Children's Homes Regulations 2001]

- The registered provider must appoint an individual to manage the home if:

  - There is no registered manager for the home and
  - The registered provider is an organisation or partnership, is not a fit person to manage a children's home or is not or does not intend to be in fill-time day to day charge of the home

- Where the registered provider appoints a person to manage the children's home, s/he must immediately give notice to CSCI of:

  - The name of the person so appointed and
  - The date on which the appointment is to take effect

Registered Person – General Requirements [Reg. 9 Children's Homes Regulations 2001]

- The registered provider and the registered manager must, having regard to the home's size, statement of purpose, and number and needs of residents (including those arising from disability) carry on/manage the home with sufficient care, competence and skill.

- From time to time, so as to ensure sufficient experience and skills necessary for carrying on the home, appropriate training must be completed by:

- The registered provider (if s/he is an individual)
- The responsible individual (and the responsibility for ensuring this rests with the organisation which engages her/him)
- (Where relevant) 1 member of any partnership

■ The registered manager must also undertake from time to time such training as is appropriate to ensure s/he has the experience and skills necessary for managing the children's home.

Notification of Offences [Reg. 10 Children's Homes Regulations 2001]

■ Where the registered person or the responsible individual is convicted of any criminal offence in England or Wales or elsewhere, s/he must immediately give notice to CSCI of the:

- Date and place of the conviction
- Offence of which s/he was convicted
- Penalty imposed

Welfare of Children [Regs. 11–24]

Promotion of Welfare [Reg. 11 Children's Homes Regulations 2001]

- The registered person must ensure that the home is conducted so as to:

  - Promote and make proper provision for the welfare of residents
  - Make proper provision for care, education, supervision and where appropriate treatment of residents

- The registered person must make suitable arrangements to ensure the home is conducted, with respect to children accommodated there:

  - In a manner which respects their privacy and dignity
  - With due regard to their sex, religious persuasion, racial origin and cultural and linguistic background and any disability

Child's Placement Plan [Reg.12 Children's Homes Regulations 2001]

- The registered person must, before providing accommodation (or if that is not reasonably practicable, as soon as possible thereafter), prepare in consultation with the placing authority a written 'placement plan' setting out:

Welfare of Children

- How, day to day, s/he will be cared for and her/his welfare safeguarded and promoted by the home
- Arrangements made for her/his health care and education
- Any arrangements made for contact with her/his parents, relatives and friends

■ The registered person must keep under review and revise the placement plan as necessary

■ In preparing or reviewing the plan, the registered person must, so far as practicable given child's age and understanding, seek and take account of her/his views.

■ The registered person must so far as is practicable:

- Ensure that the plan is consistent with any plan for care of child prepared by the placing authority and
- Comply with requests made by the placing authority to provide information about the child and provide a suitable representative to attend any meetings it holds

Food Provided [Reg. 13 Children's Homes Regulations 2001]

■ The registered person must ensure that the children accommodated are provided with access to fresh drinking water at all times and food which is:

- Served in adequate quantities at appropriate intervals
- Properly prepared, wholesome and nutritious
- Suitable for their needs and meets reasonable preferences
- Is sufficiently varied

■ The registered person must ensure any special dietary need of an accommodated child due to her/his health, religious persuasion, racial origin or cultural background is met.

Provision of Clothing, Pocket Money & Personal Necessities [Reg. 14 Children's Homes Regulations 2001]

■ The registered person must ensure that the needs and reasonable preferences of each resident for clothing, including footwear and personal necessities are met.

■ The registered person must provide residents with such sums of money for occasional personal expenses as are appropriate to their age and understanding.

Contact & Access to Communication [Reg. 15 Children's Homes Regulations 2001]

■ The registered person must (unless exceptions specified in the final paragraph below apply) promote contact of each child with her/his parents, relatives and friends in accordance with arrangements in the placement plan.

Welfare of Children

- Except in the case of a certified 'refuge', (when they may be at a different address) the registered person must ensure suitable facilities are provided within the home for any resident to meet privately at any reasonable time her/his parents, relatives and friends and the following individuals:

  - Any solicitor/other adviser/advocate for the child
  - Any CAFCASS officer appointed for her/him
  - Any social worker assigned to the child by the placing authority
  - Any person appointed in connection with an investigation of a complaint
  - Any independent visitor
  - Any person authorised by CSCI
  - Any person authorised by the local authority in whose area the home is situated
  - Any person authorised by Secretary of State to inspect the home and the children there

- The registered person must ensure that residents are provided at all reasonable times with access to the following facilities which they may use in private without reference to persons working in the home:

  - A telephone on which to make and receive calls
  - A capacity to send and receive post and (where available) e-mails

- The registered person must ensure any resident is provided with access to such aids and equipment which s/he may require as a result of her/his disability in order to facilitate communication with others.

■ The registered person **may** [Reg. 15(6)–(7) Children's Homes Regulations 2001] impose such restriction, prohibition or condition upon a child's contact or access to communications which s/he is satisfied is necessary for the purpose of safeguarding or promoting the welfare of the child in question only if:

- The child's placing authority consents to the imposition of the measure or
- The measure is imposed in an emergency and full details are given to the placing authority with 24 hours of its imposition

NB. Reg. 15 is subject to the provisions of any relevant court order relating to contact between child and any person [Reg. 15(8) Children's Homes Regulations 2001].

Arrangements for Protection of Children [Reg. 16 Children's Homes Regulations 2001]

■ The registered person must prepare and implement a written policy which:

- Is intended to safeguard children accommodated in the children's home from abuse or neglect and
- Sets out the procedure to be followed in the event of any allegation or abuse or neglect

■ The child protection procedures must in particular provide for:

Welfare of Children

- Liaison and co-operation with any local authority which is or may be making child protection enquiries in relation to any resident
- Prompt referral to the local authority in whose area the home is situated, of any allegation of abuse or neglect affecting any accommodated child
- Notification (in accordance with Reg. 30) of instigation and outcome of any child protection enquiries involving any child accommodated to CSCI and the child's placing authority
- Written records to be kept of any allegations of abuse or neglect, and of any action taken in response
- Consideration to be given to measures which may be necessary to protect children in the home following an allegation of abuse or neglect
- A requirement for persons working at the home to report any concerns about the welfare or safety of an accommodated child to either the registered person, a police officer, an officer of CSCI, an officer of the local authority where the home is situated or an officer of the NSPCC
- Arrangements to be made for persons working in the home and residents to have access at all times and in an appropriate form, to information that would enable them (in the event that they were concerned about a resident child's welfare or safety) to contact the local authority where the home is, or CSCI

- The registered person must also prepare and implement as required a:
  - Written policy for the prevention of bullying in the home which must in particular set out the procedure for dealing with an allegation of bullying
  - Procedure to be followed when any resident is absent without permission

Behaviour Management, Discipline and Restraint [Reg. 17 Children's Homes Regulations 2001]

- No measure of control, restraint or discipline which is excessive, unreasonable or contrary to the prohibited measures listed below may be used at any time on a resident.

- The registered person must prepare and implement a written 'behaviour management policy' which sets out the:
  - Measures of control, restraint and disciple which may be used in the home and
  - Means whereby appropriate behaviour is to be promoted in the home

- The registered person must keep under review and where appropriate revise the behaviour management policy and notify CSCI within 28 days of any such revision.

- Registered person must ensure that within 24 hours of use of any measure of control, restraint or discipline in a home, a written record is made in a volume kept for the purpose, of:

- The name of the child concerned
- Details of behaviour leading to use of measure
- A description of the measure used
- Date, time and location of the use of the measure and (where applicable) the duration of any restraint
- The name of the person using the measure and of any other person present
- The effectiveness and any consequences of the use of the measure and
- The signature of a person authorised by the registered provider to make the record

■ The following are prohibited as disciplinary measures on children accommodated in a children's home:

- Any form of corporal punishment
- Any punishment relating to the consumption or deprivation of food or drink
- Any restriction (other than one imposed by a court or in accordance with Reg. 15 – contact and access to communications) on child's contact with or visits from parent, relative or friend, communications with any persons listed in Reg. 15 or access to a help-line providing counselling for children
- Any requirement that the child wear distinctive or inappropriate clothes
- The use or withholding of medication or medical or dental treatment

- Intentional deprivation of sleep
- Imposition of any financial penalty other than a requirement for payment of a reasonable sum (which may be by installments) by way of reparation
- Any intimate physical examination of the child
- The withholding of any aids or equipment needed by a disabled child
- Any measure which involves any child in the imposition of any measure against any other child or group punishment for an individual's misbehaviour

■ Nothing in the above list prohibits the:

- Taking of any by action by, or in accordance with the instructions of a doctor or dentist which is necessary to protect the health of a child
- Taking of any action immediately necessary to prevent injury to any person or serious damage to property or
- Imposition of a requirement that a child wears distinctive clothing for sporting purposes or for purposes connected with her/his education or with any organisation whose members customarily wear uniforms e.g. guides or scouts.

Education, Employment & Leisure Activity [Reg. 18 Children's Homes Regulations 2001]

■ The registered person must promote the educational attainment of children accommodated in a children's home, in particular by ensuring that:

- Children make use of educational facilities appropriate to their age, aptitude, needs, interests and potential
- The routine of the home is organised so as to further children's participation in education, including private study and
- Effective links are maintained with any schools attended by children accommodated in the home

■ The registered person must ensure that residents are:
- Encouraged to develop and pursue appropriate leisure interests and
- Provided with appropriate leisure facilities and activities

■ Where any child in a children's home has attained the age where s/he is no longer required to receive compulsory full-time education, the registered person must assist with making and implementing arrangements for her/his education, training and employment.

Religious Observance [s.19 Children's Homes Regulations 2001]

■ The registered person must ensure that each accommodated child is enabled, so far as practicable with respect her/his religious persuasion, to:
- Attend services
- Receive instruction
- Observe any requirements as to dress, diet or otherwise

Health Needs of Children [Reg. 20 Children's Homes Regulations 2001]

- The registered person must promote and protect the health of residents and in particular ensure that:
    - Each child is registered with a GP and has access to such medical, dental, nursing, psychological and psychiatric advice, treatment and other services as s/he may require
    - Each child is provided with such individual support, aids and equipment as s/he may require as result of any particular health needs or disability
    - Each child is provided with guidance, support and advice on health and personal care issues appropriate to her/his needs and wishes
    - At all times, at least 1 person on duty at the home has a suitable first aid qualification
    - Any person appointed to the position of nurse at the children's home is a registered nurse

Medicines [Reg. 21 Children's Homes Regulations 2001]

- The registered person must make suitable arrangements for the recording, handling, safekeeping, safe administration and disposal of any medicines received into the home.

- In particular the registered person must (unless it is stored by the child for whom it is intended in such a way that others are prevented from using it, and may be self-administered) ensure that:

- Any medicine kept in the home is stored in a secure place so as to prevent any resident having unsupervised access to it
- Any prescribed medicine is administered as prescribed only to the child for whom intended
- A written record is kept of the administration of any medicine to any child

Use of Surveillance [Reg. 22 Children's Homes Regulations 2001]

■ Subject to any requirements for electronic monitoring imposed by a court under any law, the registered person must ensure that electronic or mechanical monitoring devices for surveillance of children are not used in the home, except for the purpose of safeguarding and promoting the welfare of the child concerned or other residents and where the following conditions are met:

- The child's placing authority consent
- It is provided for in the child's placement plan
- So far as practicable in the light of her/his age and understanding, the child in question is informed in advance of the intention to use the measure and
- The measure is not more restrictive than necessary, having regard to the child's needs for privacy

Welfare of Children

Hazards & Safety [Reg. 23 Children's Homes Regulations 2001]

- The registered person must ensure that:
  - All parts of the home to which the children have access are as far as reasonably practicable free from hazards to their safety
  - Any activities in which children participate are so far as reasonably practicable free from avoidable risks
  - Unnecessary risks to the health or safety of children accommodated in the home are identified and so far as possible eliminated
  - Suitable arrangements are made for persons working at the home to be trained in first aid

Complaints & Representations [Reg. 24 Children's Homes Regulations 2001]

- The Children Act 1989 (Representations Procedure (England) Regulations 2006 revoked and replaced the Representations Procedure (Children) Regulations 1991 and reflected the changes made by the Adoption and Children Act 2002 and the Health and Social Care (Community Health and Standards) Act 2003 to the provisions for the procedures under the Children Act 1989 for considering representations, including complaints.

- The major differences between the old and the new regulations are: imposition of a general 12 month time limit on making representations, extension of local authority functions about which representations can be made under s. 26 to include Part IV and V as well as Part III of CA 1989), introduction of a requirement on local authorities to attempt (time limited) informal resolution of all representations under that Act, an obligation to provide relevant complainants (those in need or looked after) with information about advocacy services and a requirement to provide a wholly independent panel for those who choose to pursue their complaint to the 3rd stage of the procedure.

NB. CAE's 'Personal Guide to the Children Act 1989 in the context of the Human Rights Act 1998' includes more detail about the revised procedures.

Staffing [Regs. 25–27]

Numbers & Fitness [Regs. 25, 26 Children's Homes Regulations 2001]

- The registered person must ensure that there is at all times a sufficient number of suitably qualified, competent and experienced persons working at the home, having regard to the:
  - Size of the home, its statement of purpose and the number and needs (including any arising from any disability) of residents
  - Need to safeguard and promote the health and welfare of the residents

- The registered person must ensure that the employment of any persons on a temporary basis at the home will not prevent the children from receiving such continuity of care as is reasonable to meet their needs.

- The registered person must not, unless the person in question is fit to work at a children's home:
  - Employ a person to work at the home or
  - Allow a person who is employed by someone other than the registered person to work at the home in a position in which s/he may in the course of her/his duties have regular contact with residents

- A person is not fit to work at a children's home unless:

Staffing

- S/he is of integrity and good character
- Has the qualifications, skills and experience necessary for the work s/he is to perform
- Is physically and mentally fit for the purposes of the work to be performed and
- Full and satisfactory information is available about the person as per paras. 1–6 of Sch. 2 Children's Homes Regulations 2001 (prior to the implementation of ss.113 & 115 Police Act 1997) and paras. 1 and 3–7 (following implementation)

■ The registered person must ensure that:

- Any offer of employment is subject to requirements of the final bullet point above being satisfied
- Unless the circumstances described below apply, no person starts work at a children's home until such time as those requirements have been satisfied

■ Where the following criteria apply, the registered person **may** permit a person to start work at a children's home **if:**

- S/he has taken all reasonable steps to obtain full information in respect of each of the matters listed in Sch. 2 but enquiries in relation to any matters listed in paras. 3–6 are incomplete i.e. 2 references, verification of reasons for termination of previous comparable work, evidence of relevant qualifications, full employment history
- Full and satisfactory information in respect of

that person has been obtained in relation to para. 1 Sch. 2 (proof of identity including a recent photo) and
- Full and satisfactory information in respect of that person has been obtained in relation to para. 2 of Sch. 2 (except where any provision of the Police Act 1997 has not been brought into force) and
- (Where the Police Act 1997 has been brought into force) full and satisfactory information in respect of that person has been obtained in relation to para. 7 of Sch. 2 (all convictions and cautions)
- The registered person considers that the circumstances are exceptional and pending receipt of satisfactory information, s/he ensures that the person is appropriately supervised while carrying out her/his duties

■ The registered person must also take reasonable steps to ensure that any person, other than one already specified above who works at a children's home is appropriately supervised while carrying out her/his duties.

Employment of Staff [Reg. 27 Children's Homes Regulations 2001]

■ The registered person must:

- Ensure all permanent appointments are subject to the satisfactory completion of a period of probation and
- Provide all employees with a job description

Staffing

- The registered person must operate a disciplinary procedure which, in particular:

  - Provides for the suspension of an employee where necessary in the interests of the safety or welfare of children accommodated in the home
  - Provides that the failure on the part of an employee to report an incident of abuse, or suspected abuse, of a resident to an appropriate person (the registered person, an officer of CSCI or local authority in which home is situated, a police officer) is a ground on which disciplinary proceedings may be instituted

- The registered person must ensure that all persons employed by her/him:

  - Receive appropriate training, supervision and appraisal and
  - Are enabled from time to time to obtain further qualifications appropriate to the work the perform

Records [Regs. 28-30]

Children's Case Records [Reg. 28 Children's Homes Regulations 2001]

- The registered person must maintain in respect of each accommodated child a permanent record which:

  - Includes the information, documents and records specified in Sch. 3 (see below) relating to that child
  - Is kept up to date and
  - Is signed and dated by the author of each entry

- Sch. 3 specifies the following:

  - Current and any previous name (other than a name used prior to adoption)
  - Sex and date of birth
  - Racial origin, cultural and linguistic background
  - Address immediately prior to entering the home
  - Name, address and telephone number of child's placing authority
  - Statutory provision (if any) under which s/he is provided with accommodation
  - Name, address, phone number and religion (if any) of child's parents
  - Name, address and phone number of her/his social worker from the placing authority
  - Date and circumstance of any absence from the home (authorised or not) and where resident went

- Date and reason for visit to the child whilst in the home
- A copy of any statement of special educational needs being maintained under s.324 Education Act 1996 and details
- Date and circumstance of any measures of control, restraint or discipline used on the child
- Name and address of any school or college attended or of an employer
- Any special dietary or health needs
- Name, address and telephone number of any school or college attended by the child, and of any employer of the child
- Every school report received while resident
- Arrangements for, including any restrictions on, contact between child and parents, and any other person
- A copy of any plan for the care of the child prepared by the placing authority and of the placement plan
- Date and result of any review of the placing authority's plan for the care of the child, or of her/his placement plan
- Name and address of resident's general practitioner and dentist
- Details of any accident or serious illness involving the resident
- Immunisation, illness, allergy or medical examination details, any medical or dental needs or treatment of the child
- Details of any health examination or

developmental test conducted with respect to the child at, or in connection with her/his school
- Details of any medicine kept for the child in the home, including any which the child is permitted to self-administer and details of administration of any medicine to her/him
- The dates on which money or valuables deposited by or on behalf of a resident for safekeeping and dates on which any money is withdrawn and any valuable returned
- The address and type of establishment or accommodation to which the child goes when s/he ceases to be accommodated in the home

■ The above record may not be disclosed to any person except in accordance with:

- Any legal provision which may make access to it lawful or
- Any court order authorising access to such records

■ The above record must be:

- Kept securely in the home so long as the child to whom it relates is accommodated there and
- Thereafter retained in a place of security for at least 75 years from date of birth, or if s/he dies before 18 years of age, for 15 years from date of death

Other Records [Reg. 29 & Sch. 4 Children's Homes Regulations 2001]

- The registered person must maintain and keep up to date, in the home the following records:

  - Date of child's admission to the home
  - Date on which child ceased to be accommodated
  - Address prior to being accommodated in the home and address on leaving the home
  - Placing authority and statutory provisions (if any) under which the child is accommodated
  - A record showing for each person working at the home full name, sex, date of birth, home address, qualifications relevant to and experience of work involving children
  - Whether s/he works at the home full or part-time (paid or not) and if part-time the average number of hours worked per week
  - Whether s/he resides at the home
  - A record of any persons who reside or work at any time at the home, who are not mentioned in the records kept in accordance with the first two bullet points above
  - A record of all accidents occurring in the home, or to children whilst accommodated by the home
  - A record of the receipt, disposal and administration of any medicine to any child
  - A record of every fire drill or alarm test conducted, with details of any deficiency in either the procedure or equipment concerned, taught with details of the steps taken to remedy that deficiency

Records

- A record of all money deposited by a child for safekeeping, together with the date on which that money was withdrawn, or the date of its return
- A record of all valuables deposited by a child their date of return
- Records of all accounts kept in the children's home
- A record of menus served
- A copy of the staff duty roster of persons working at the home and a record of the actual rosters worked
- A daily log of events occurring in the home
- A record of all visitors to the home and to children accommodated, including the names of visitors and reasons for the visit

■ The above records must be retained for at least 15 years from the date of the last entry, except for records of menus which need be kept for only 1 year.

Notifiable Events [Reg. 30 Children's Homes Regulations 2001]

■ If any of the events below takes place, the registered person must without delay notify the persons indicated.

■ If a resident dies the following people must be notified and provided with all known details:

- CSCI
- Placing authority

- Secretary of Sate
- Local authority
- Health authority

■ A referral to the Secretary of State pursuant to s.2(1)(a) of Protection of Children Act 1999 of an individual working in the home must be referred to the:

- CSCI
- Placing authority

■ A serious illness or serious accident sustained by a resident must be notified to the:

- CSCI
- Placing authority

■ An outbreak of any infectious disease which in the opinion of doctor attending residents is sufficiently serious must be notified to the:

- CSCI
- Placing authority
- Health authority

■ An allegation that a child accommodated at the home has committed a serious offence must be notified to the:

- Placing authority
- Police

■ Involvement or suspected involvement of a resident in prostitution must be notified to the:

- CSCI
- Placing authority
- Local authority
- Police

■ A serious incident necessitating calling the police to the home must be notified to the:

- CSCI
- Placing authority

■ Absconding by a child accommodated at the home must be notified to the:

- Placing authority

■ Any serious complaint about the home or persons working there must be notified to the:

- CSCI
- Placing authority

■ Instigation and outcome of any child protection enquiries involving a resident must be notified to the:

- CSCI
- Placing authority

■ The registered person must also without delay, notify the parent of any child accommodated in the home of any significant incident affecting the child's welfare unless to do so is not reasonably practicable or would place the child's welfare at risk.

Premises [Regs. 31 & 32]

Fitness of Premises [Reg. 31 Children's Homes Regulations 2001]

- The registered person must not use premises as a children's home unless they are in a location, and of a physical design and layout, which are suitable for the purpose of achieving the aims and objectives set out in the home's statement of purpose.

- The registered person must ensure that all parts of the home used by children are:
  - Adequately lit, heated and ventilated
  - Secure from unauthorised access
  - Suitably furnished and equipped
  - Of sound construction and kept in good structural repair externally and internally
  - Kept clean and reasonably decorated and maintained
  - Equipped with what is reasonably necessary and adapted as necessary, to meet the needs arising from her/his disability of any disabled resident so as to enable her/him to live as normal a life as possible

- The registered person must ensure the home is kept free from offensive odours and make suitable arrangements for disposal of general and clinical waste.

Premises

- The registered person must ensure there are within the home, for use by residents in conditions of appropriate privacy (taking account of their numbers and sex) a sufficient number of:

  - Wash basins, baths and showers supplied with hot and cold running water
  - Lavatories

- The registered person must provide for the number and needs of residents:

  - Sufficient and suitable kitchen equipment, crockery, cutlery and utensils
  - Adequate facilities for preparation and storage of food
  - So far as is practicable, adequate facilities for children to prepare their own food if they so wish and are of an age and ability to do so

- The registered person must ensure that there are within a home, adequate facilities for laundering linen and clothing and for children wishing to do so, to wash, dry and iron their own clothes.

- The registered person must ensure that there is provided within a home:

  - Adequate communal space for sitting, recreation and dining
  - Such facilities for private study as are appropriate to the age and educational needs of residents

- The registered person must ensure that each resident is provided with sleeping accommodation which is:

Premises

- Suitable to her/his needs including need for privacy
- Equipped with furniture, storage facilities, lighting, bedding and other furnishings including window and floor coverings suitable to her/his needs

■ The registered person must ensure that no child shares a bedroom with an adult, nor (except in the case of siblings) a child who is of the opposite sex or of a significantly different age to her/him

■ The registered person must provide for persons working at the home:

- Suitable facilities and accommodation, other than sleeping accommodation including those for the purposes of changing and storage
- Sleeping accommodation where this is necessary for work purposes

Fire Precautions [Reg. 32 Children's Homes Regulations 2001]

■ The registered person must, after consultation with the fire authority:

- Take adequate precautions against the risk of fire including the provision of fire equipment
- Provide adequate means of escape
- Make adequate arrangements for detecting, containing and extinguishing fire
- Make adequate arrangements for giving warnings of fire

Premises

- Make adequate arrangements for evacuation in the event of a fire
- Make adequate arrangements for the maintenance of all fire equipment
- Make adequate arrangements for reviewing fire precautions and testing fire equipment at suitable intervals
- Make arrangements for persons working at the home to receive suitable training in fire prevention
- Ensure by means of fire drills and practices at suitable intervals, that those working at the home, and so far as practicable, the residents, are aware of the procedure to be followed in case of fire

Management of Home [Regs.33–36]

Visits by Registered Provider [Reg. 33 Children's Homes Regulations 2001]

- Where the registered provider is an individual, but is not in day to day charge of the home, s/he must visit in accordance with this regulation.

- Where the registered provider is an organisation or a partnership, the home must be visited in accordance with this regulation by:
  - The responsible individual or one of the partners as the case may be
  - Another of the directors or other persons responsible for the management of the organisation or partnership
  - An employee of the organisations or partnership not directly concerned with the conduct of the home

- The visits referred to above must be at least monthly and be unannounced.

- The person carrying out the visit must:
  - Interview, with their consent and in private such of the residents, parents, relatives and persons working at the home as appears necessary to form an opinion of the standard of care provided
  - Inspect the premises, its daily log of events and records of any complaints

- Prepare a written report on the conduct of the home

■ The registered provider must supply a copy of the above report to the:

- CSCI
- Registered manager of the home and
- Where the registered provider is an organisation, to each of the directors or other persons responsible for management of the organisation, and where the registered provider is a partnership, to each of the partners

Review of Quality of Care [Reg. 34 Children's Homes Regulations 2001]

■ The registered person must establish and maintain a system for monitoring at appropriate intervals, matters set out in Sch. 6 (reproduced below) and for improving the quality of care:

- For each resident, compliance with placing authority's plan for care of child (where applicable) and the placement plan
- Deposit and issue of money and other valuable handed in for safekeeping
- Daily menus
- All accidents and injuries sustained in the home or by children accommodated there
- Any illness of residents
- Complaints in relation to residents and their outcomes

- Any allegations or suspicions of abuse with respect to residents and the outcome of any investigation
- Staff recruitment records and conduct of required checks for new workers in the home
- Visitors to the home and to children in the home
- Notifications of events listed in Sch. 5
- Any unauthorised absence from the home of a resident
- Use of measures of control, restraint and discipline in respect of children accommodated there
- Risk assessments for health and safety purposes and subsequent action taken
- Medicines, medical treatment and first aid administered to any child accommodated
- In the case of qualifying school, the standard of educational provision
- Duty rosters of persons working at the home and rosters actually worked
- Home's daily log of events
- Fire drills and tests of alarms and of fire equipment
- Records of appraisals of employees
- Minutes of staff meetings

■ The registered person must supply CSCI with a report of any review s/he conducts and make a copy available on request to children accommodated in the home, their parents and placing authorities.

Regulations & Guidance [Reg. 35 Children's Homes Regulations 2001]

- Registered person must ensure a copy of the Children's Homes Regulations 2001 (and any amendments to them) as well as the national minimum standards are kept in the home and made available on request to:
  - Any person working in the home
  - Any child accommodated in the home
  - The parent of any child accommodated in the home

Financial Position [Reg. 36 Children's Homes Regulations 2001]

- The registered provider must carry on the home in such a manner as is likely to ensure it will be financially viable for the purpose of achieving the aims and objectives set out in its statement of purpose.

- The registered person must:
  - Ensure that adequate accounts are maintained and kept up to date in respect of the home
  - Supply a copy to CSCI at its request

- The registered person must provide CSCI with such information as it may require for the purpose of considering financial viability of the home, including:
  - Annual certified accounts
  - A bank reference

- Information about financing and financial resources of the home
- Where the registered provider is a company, information as to any of its associated companies
- A certificate of insurance covering death, injury, public liability, damage or other loss

Miscellaneous [Regs. 37–43]

Notice of Absence [Reg. 37 Children's Homes Regulations 2001]

- Where registered provider (if s/he is in day to day charge) or registered manager proposes to be absent for a continuous period of 28 days or more, the registered person must give written notice to CSCI.

- Except in an emergency, notice must be given no later than 1 month before the proposed absence, or within such shorter period as may be agreed with CSCI.

- The notice must specify with respect to the absence:
  - Its length or expected length and reasons for it
  - Arrangements made for running the home
  - Name, address and qualifications of the person who will be responsible for the home during the absence
  - (In the case of absence of registered manager) arrangements which have been/proposed to be made for appointing another person to manage the home during the absence, including proposed date by which the appointment is to be made

- Where the absence arises as a result of an emergency, the registered person must give notice of the absence within 1 week of its occurrence specifying the matters listed in bullet points above.

Miscellaneous

- Where the registered provider (if s/he is in day to day charge of the home) or the registered manager has been absent from the home for a continuous period of 28 days or more and CSCI has not been given notice of the absence, the registered person must without delay give notice in writing to CSCI specifying the matters listed in the bullet points above.

- The registered person must notify CSCI of the return to duty of the registered provider or (as the case may be) the registered manager not later than 7 days after the date of her/his return.

Notice of Changes [Reg. 38 Children's Homes Regulations 2001]

- The registered person must give written notice to CSCI as soon as practicable to do so if any of the following events take place or are proposed to take place:

  - A person other than the registered person carries on or manages the home
  - A person ceases to carry on the home
  - Where the registered provider is an individual,/she changes her/his name
  - Where the registered provide is a partnership, there is any change in the membership of the partnership
  - Where the registered provider is an organisation the name or address of the organisations is changed, there is any change of director,

manager, secretary or similar officer, there is to be any change in identity of the responsible individual
- Where the registered provider is a company, a receiver, manager, liquidator or provisional liquidator is appointed
- The premises of the home are significantly altered or extended, or additional premises are acquired

■ Any receiver/liquidator/provisional liquidator/trustee in bankruptcy who is appointed must notify CSCI as described in Reg. 39.

Death of Registered Person [Reg. 40]

■ If more than 1 person is registered in respect of a home and a registered person dies, the other registered person must without delay notify CSCI in writing.

■ If only 1 person is registered and s/he dies, her/his personal representative must notify CSCI in writing without delay and (within 28 days) of her/his intentions regarding future running of the home.

■ The personal representative of the deceased registered provider may carry on the home without being registered for a period not exceeding 28 days or for any period (up to a maximum of 1 year) as may be determined and confirmed in writing by CSCI.

NB. In such circumstances, the personal representative must appoint a person to take full-time day to day charge during any period in which they carry on the home without being registered with respect to it.

Offences [Reg. 41 Children's Homes Regulations 2001]

- A contravention or failure to comply with the provisions of Regulations 4 to 38 is an offence.

- CSCI must not bring proceedings against a person in respect of any contravention or failure to comply with these regulations unless:
  - S/he is a registered person (or is temporarily not required to be registered as per Regulation 40)
  - Notice has been given as described below
  - The period specified in the notice has expired
  - The person contravenes or fails to comply with any provisions of the regulations mentioned in the notice

- Where CSCI considers that the registered person has contravened or failed to comply with any of the provisions of Regulations 4–38, it may serve a notice on the registered person specifying:
  - In what respect in its opinion the registered person has contravened or is contravening any of the regulations, or has failed or is failing to comply with the requirements of any of the regulations
  - What action, in the opinion of CSCI, the registered person should take so as to comply with any of those regulations

Miscellaneous

- The period, not exceeding 3 months, within which the registered person should take action

NB. CSCI may bring proceedings against a person who was once, but no longer is, a registered person, in respect of failure to comply with Reg. 28(3) storage of case records and 29(2) storage of other records [Reg. 41 Children's Homes Regulations 2001].

Compliance with Regulations [Reg. 42 Children's Homes Regulations 2001]

■ Where there is more than 1 registered person for a home, compliance by 1 registered person with anything required by these regulations is sufficient.

Registration Regulations

Applications [Regs. 3–7 NCSC (Registration) Regulations 2001 as amended by The Health and Social Care (Community Health and Standards) Act 2003 (Commission for Healthcare Audit and Inspection and Commission for Social Care Inspection) (Transitional and Consequential Provisions) Order 2004

- An application for registration must be:
  - In writing on a form approved by CSCI
  - Sent or delivered to the CSCI
  - Be accompanied by a recent photograph of the responsible person
  - Give information as described in Reg. 3

- An applicant must supply in writing to CSCI details of any 'spent' convictions s/he has.

- The responsible person must attend an interview to enable CSCI to determine whether s/he is fit to carry on or manage the home.

- The applicant must give written notice to CSCI of any changes after the application is made and before it is determined:
  - Of any change of name or address of applicant or any responsible person
  - Where the applicant is a partnership, of any change of membership of the partnership
  - Where the applicant is an organisation, any change of director, manager, secretary or other person responsible for the management of the organisation
- Reg. 7 sets out obligations with respect to information required about staff engaged after an application is made and before it is determined.

Register & Certificate
[Regs. 8, 9 & 10]

- CSCI must maintain a register in respect of children's homes and other establishments specified in s.4(8)(a) and (9)(a) CSA 2000.

- Each register must contain particulars specified in part 1 and register details in Part 111 of the registration regulations and the contents of a certificate issued by CSCI will contain particulars specified in Reg.9 of those.

NB. If a person's registration is cancelled, s/he must, not later than the day on which decision/order cancelling it takes effect, return it to CSCI by delivering/sending it registered post or recorded delivery. Failure to comply is an offence.

Conditions & Reports & Cancellation of Registration [Regs.12–15]

- Regulation 12 details the process for an application to vary or remove a condition in relation to registration.

- Regulation 13 addresses financial viability and Regulations 14 & 15 specify grounds for cancellation of registration (other grounds for cancellation are contained in s.14 CSA 2000).

- Regulation 15 provides for the registered person to apply for her/his registration to be cancelled.

Fees & Frequency of Inspections

NB. All the fees described below are likely to be raised annually in April.

Registration Fees [Reg. 3 CSCI (Fees & Frequency of Inspections) Regulations 2004]

- An application for registration by a person seeking to be registered as a person who carries on/provides the home:
  - £1,584-00

- An application for registration by a person who is seeking to be registered as a person who manages the home:
  - £432-00

- For an application in respect of a children's home for 3 or fewer residents:
  - By a person seeking to be registered as a person who provides it £432-00
  - By a person seeking to be registered as a person who manages it £ nil

Variation Fees [CSCI (Fees & Frequency of Inspection (Amendment) Regulations 2006]

- Variation fee for application by registered provider under s.15(1)(a) CSA 2000 – (variation or removal of any condition for time being in force in relation to the registration):

    - £1,093-00

- For an application under s.15(1)(a) in respect of an establishment which is a 'small establishment', for an application by a person seeking to be registered as a person who carries on the establishment:

    - Variation fee of £596-00

NB. In a case where the variation of a condition is a minor variation, the variation fee will be £99-00. A minor variation is one is one in which in the opinion of CSCI, if the application for the variation were granted, would involve no material alteration in the register kept by it [Reg. 4(4) CSCI (Fees and Frequency of Inspection) Regulations 2004.

Annual Fees [Reg. 5 CSCI (Fees & Frequency of Inspections) Regulations 2004]

- A registered provider or relevant person:
  - Children's Home £994-00 flat rate + £99-00 per approved place from 4 – 29 places inclusive, and £99-00 per subsequent approved place

NB. For a 'small establishment' i.e. 3 or fewer residents the annual fee is limited to the flat rate specified above [Reg.5 (3)].

Frequency of Inspection [Reg. 6 CSCI (Fees & Frequency of Inspections) Regulations 2004]

- **Children's Home** A minimum of 2 inspections in every 12 month period

    NB. Any inspection may be unannounced [Reg 6 (5) CSCI (Fees & Frequency of Inspection) Regulations 2004.

    The DfES is currently consulting upon changes to the required frequency of inspections.

National Minimum Standards: Children's Homes

Introduction

- The standards are qualitative, in that they focus on the impact on the individual resident of the home's facilities and services. They are also intended to be measurable and are grouped as follows:
  - Planning for care
  - Quality of care
  - Complaints and protection
  - Care and control
  - Environment
  - Staffing
  - Management and administration
  - Specialist provision

- Each standard is preceded by a statement of the desired outcome for service users and the full set of numbered paragraphs of each standard must be met in order to achieve compliance with the standards.

- Regulations and primary legislation to which each standard is linked are cited in the black title box and unless otherwise specified, refer to the Children's Homes Regulations 2001 and the Children Act 1989 respectively.

Standard 1: Written Statement of Purpose [links to Regs. 4 & 5].

Outcome: Children and young people are guided through and know what services they can expect from the home, how they will be cared for, with whom they are likely to share and a clear statement of how the home operates is available for parents and others needing this information.

- **1.1 The home has a written statement of purpose and a children's guide which accurately describes what the home sets out to do for children it accommodates, and the manner in which care is provided**

- 1.2 The Statement of Purpose provides all the information required in Schedule 1 of the Children's Homes Regulations 2001 – S.I.2001 No. 3967, in a form that can be understood by placing social workers, staff and any parent or person with parental responsibility for a child. All those working in the home are aware of the contents of the Statement of Purpose, and a copy is easily accessible.

- 1.3 The children's guide to the home is in a form/forms appropriate to age and understanding of residents. For some children e.g. young, disabled or those for whom English is not the preferred language, alternative methods of communicating the guide are sought, e.g. Makaton, pictures, tapes

Standard 1: Written Statement of Purpose

recording, translation. The guide is provided on admission and includes a summary of what the home sets out to do for children, information on how a child can secure access to an independent advocate and make a complaint.

- 1.4 The home's policies, procedures and any written guidance to staff accurately reflect the Statement of Purpose.

- 1.5 The registered person (in case of the local authority, the elected member) formally approves the Statement of Purpose of the home and reviews, updates and modifies it where necessary, at least annually. Proposed significant changes or modifications are notified to the Commission before implementation.

Standard 2: Placement Plans [links to Reg. 12]

Outcome: Children have their needs assessed effectively and comprehensively, and written placement plans outline how these needs will be met and are implemented. Children in the home are appropriately placed there.

- **2.1 The placement plan for each child sets out clearly assessed needs of the child, objectives of the placement, how these are to be met by the registered person on a day to day basis, the contribution to be made by the staff and how the effectiveness of the placement is to be assessed in relation to each major element of the plan. The plan includes:**
  - Health needs and health promotion
  - Care needs including safeguarding and promoting welfare
  - Physical and emotion needs
  - Education needs and attainment targets
  - Cultural, religious, language and racial needs and how they will be met
  - Leisure needs
  - Contact arrangements with family, friends and significant others

- The placement plan is consistent with any plan for the care of the child prepared by the placing

Standard 2: Placement Plans

authority (where other plans cover the above, the placement plan may simply refer to existing documents without any need for duplication).

- 2.2 Each child's placement plan is monitored by a key worker within the home who ensures implementation in the day-to-day care of that child. The key worker also provides individual guidance and support to the child and makes time available to enable her/him to seek guidance, advice and support. Where homes do not use the key worker scheme, responsibility passes to the registered person or another nominated staff member.

- 2.3 The child's wishes are sought and taken into account in the selection of their key worker and her/his wishes taken into account if the child requests a change of key worker or other such person as noted in 2.2.

- 2.4 Support for a disabled child with communication difficulties is provided to help her/him become active in making decisions about her/his life.

- 2.5 The registered person frequently seeks the views of individual children, their parents (unless inappropriate) and contact person in their placing authority on content and implementation of placement plan, and takes these into account in initiating and amending the plan.

- 2.6 Children in the home know the content of their overall care plans and placement plan, according to their level of understanding.

Standard 3: Reviews [links to Reg.12]

Outcome: Children's needs and development are reviewed regularly in the light of their care and progress at the home.

- **3.1 The registered person contributes effectively to each child's placement plan and child in care review, and ensures that the child participates as far as is feasible in the review process. S/ he ensures the agreed outcome of reviews is reflected as necessary in day-to-day care of the child as described in placement plan.**

- 3.2 The registered person ensures the child is enabled, as far as is feasible, to be involved in the review process before, during and after the meeting, including agreeing time and place of reviews, assists her/him to contribute fully to the process; and assists in line with the child's wishes in the involvement of an advocate.

- 3.3 The registered person contacts placing authorities to request emergency and statutory reviews when due for any child, if not arranged by the placing authority.

- 3.4 Results of all reviews are recorded on the child's file, and individuals responsible for pursuing actions at the home arising from reviews are clearly identified.

Standard 3: Reviews

- 3.5 The home's staff contribute effectively to all reviews on progress and any difficulties of the child in placement; attend meetings concerning the child at the request of the placing authority; provide relevant information on request to the child's placing authority; and specifically highlight the achievements of children.

- 3.6 Written copies of their reviews are made available to children, and they are assisted to understand and store them safely. Where necessary, reviews are translated or communicated in a form best suited to the child.

Standard 4: Contact [links to Reg. 15]

Outcome: Children are able to maintain constructive contact with their families, friends and other people who play a significant role in their lives.

- **4.1 Children are provided with practical support for constructive contact with parents, family and other significant people, and are encouraged to maintain contact.**

- 4.2 Contact arrangements are discussed at the time of the child's admission and detailed in the placement plan. Any restrictions on contact for the protection of the child are clear. Where there are no restrictions, contact by visits, telephone, e-mail, if available and letters are all facilitated.

- 4.3 Written guidance is provided for staff which clarifies:
    - The rights of a child, parents and others to maintain contact
    - Where necessary, to supervise visits in order to safeguard the child or other children in the home
    - When and how to encourage parents, relatives and friends to take part in activities in the home.

Standard 5: Moving in and Leaving the Home [links to Reg. 11, ss. 22, 61, 64 CA 1989]

Outcome: Children are able to move into and leave the home in a planned and sensitive manner.

- 5.1 There are procedures for introducing children to the home, the staff and the children living there which cover planned and, where permitted under the home's Statement of Purpose, emergency admissions.

- 5.2 The home's expectations of the child and what they can expect of staff are clearly explained, prior to admission where possible or immediately on admission, and are reiterated as often as is necessary to ensure that the child has understood them.

- 5.3 Children are encouraged to bring favourite and cherished possessions with them when they move into the home. Careful consideration is given to the possibility of pets and to bringing items of high value, if this is requested.

- 5.4 There are procedures for children leaving the home covering both planned and emergency departures.

- 5.5 On moving to or leaving the home children are provided with written and verbal information providing facts which they need and wish to have. If leaving the home is also moving to independent or semi-independent living, the home makes relevant contribution of the assessment of the young person's needs and Pathway Plan and/or leaving care plan (see standard 6).

- 5.6 The registered person does not admit children in an emergency unless this is explicitly included as a function of the home in its Statement of Purpose and the home at the time of admission is able to provide a bedroom and appropriate facilities. A review is initiated as soon as possible and never more than 72 hours later after any emergency admission to consider whether the child should remain at the home or whether a different placement is in the child's best interests.

- 5.7 Both the needs of the child concerned, and the likely effects of her/his admission upon the existing group of residents, are taken into account, and recorded in decisions on admission to the home.

- 5.8 Children are supported to express and cope with their feelings about being away from home.

Standard 6: Preparation for Leaving Care [links to ss. 22, 61 64 CA 1989]

Outcome: Children receive care which helps to prepare them for and support them into adulthood.

- The registered person ensures there is a comprehensive plan for young people preparing to leave care and to move into independent or semi-independent living, which specifies the support and assistance they will need to enable a successful transition into adulthood, and which is implemented in practice. The plan is consistent with any care plan and is consistent with and contributes to the Pathway Plan and any transition plan for those with disabilities/special educational needs.

- The registered person, in agreement with the placing authority implements the leaving care plan and any aspects of the Pathway Plan which are the home's responsibility. These plans clearly outline the arrangements for:

  - Education, training and employment
  - Securing safe and affordable accommodation
  - Support necessary for disabled people
  - Financial assistance to set up and maintain independent accommodation if applicable
  - Claiming welfare benefits where this is identified as a need and they qualify

Standard 6: Preparation for Leaving Care

- General and specialised health education and care and other specialist services such as counselling
- Maintaining existing important networks as defined by the young person, which may include the children's home
- Creating new networks of advice and support if applicable
- Appropriate leisure pursuits
- Seeking assistance should problems arise

■ 6.3 The registered person contributes to the development of the Pathway Plan and works collaboratively, where appropriate, with the young person's personal adviser in implementing the Plan.

■ 6.4 Such plans are written in agreement with the young person, who is given a copy of the plan.

■ 6.5 Leaving care plans take into account the religious, racial, linguistic and cultural background of the young person.

■ 6.6 Particular attention is paid in preparing children for leaving care to the continuing needs of the young person to:

- Develop and maintain relationships with others
- Understand their sexuality and establish positive, caring social and sexual relationships
- Develop self-esteem
- Prepare for the world of work and or further or higher education
- Develop practical, daily life knowledge and skills

Standard 6: Preparation for Leaving Care

- The daily life of the home provides opportunities for all children in the home, appropriate to the age and needs of each child, for the development of knowledge and skills needed for future independent living.

Standard 7: Support to Individual Children [links to Regs: 11, 20, ss. 22, 61 & 64 CA 1989]

Outcome: Children receive individual support when they need it.

- 7.1 All children are given individualised support in line with their needs and wishes, and children identified as having particular needs receive help, guidance and support when needed or requested.

- 7.2 The registered person ensures, so far as is feasible, the provision of individually appropriate personal, health, social and sex and relationship education for each resident child, including disabled children.

- 7.3 The registered person actively promotes the involvement of all children in the home's social group, counters isolation of individuals by others, nurtures friendship and supports those children who for any reason do not readily 'fit in' to the resident group.

- 7.4 Support is provided for any child for whom English is not her/his first language (or use alternative methods of communication), enabling communication of needs, wishes and concerns with staff and other children.

Standard 7: Support to Individual Children

- 7.5 Children are able to approach any member of staff with personal concerns, not only their key worker.

- 7.6 The registered person ensures, as far as possible, that professional services are provided where necessary to help children develop individual identity in relation to their gender, disability, religious, racial, cultural or linguistic background or sexual orientation.

- 7.7 Support and advice is provided to any child in the home who is, or has been, involved in abuse or prostitution, as a victim or in abusing others, and s/he is involved in the planning of the support programme.

- 7.8 Each child has at least one person, independent of the home and the child's placing authority, whom s/he may contact directly about personal problems or concerns with the home (e.g. advocate, children's rights officer, adult family member etc.).

- 7.9 Children are supported to take controlled risks (appropriate to age and understanding) relevant and necessary in negotiating their place in the community. Significant risks are defined in the placement plan and a risk assessment is made and recorded.

- 7.10 Children whose placement plan requires specialist external services for them receive those services in practice. Staff co-operate in implementing any programmes associated with specialist services such as speech and language therapy or physiotherapy programmes.

- 7.11 Subject to the agreement of the placing authority, relevant personal, educational and health information concerning each child is passed on to that child's subsequent placement.

- 7.12 Any specific therapeutic technique is only used with any child at the home if specified in the child's placement plan and specifically approved by the placing authority and, where the placing authority does not have parental responsibility, by the child's parent and if the safe and effective use of the technique is known to be supported by evidence. It is carried out only by, on the directions of, or under the supervision of a member of staff or other practitioner holding a current recognised qualification in the therapy concerned, whose qualification the home has verified as valid and appropriate directly with awarding body or relevant register.

- Any member of staff using such a technique is subject to supervision by a person outside the home and not responsible for the home, who is qualified and experienced in the therapy concerned.

- 7.13 Appropriate support is provided for children who are refugees or seeking asylum, taking into account the particular circumstances of flight from country of origin and the advice of specialist agencies where necessary.

Standard 8: Consultation [links to Regs. 11, 15, 34, ss. 22, 61, 64 CA 1989]

Outcome: Children are encouraged and supported to make decisions about their lives and influence the way the home is run. No child is assumed to be unable to communicate her/his views.

- **8.1 Children's opinions, and those of families or others significant to the child, are sought over key decisions likely to affect her/his daily life and future. There are systems in place for doing this e.g. written agreements, private interviews, key worker sessions, children's or house meetings, and systems reflect children's differing communication needs.**

- 8.2 Staff take into account the religious, racial, cultural and linguistic backgrounds of children and their families and any disabilities they may have.

- 8.3 Significant views, discussions and expressed opinions are recorded promptly.

- 8.4 The opinions of children on all matters affecting them are ascertained on a regular and frequent basis.

- 8.5 Children, their families and significant others, receive feedback following consultation.

Standard 8: Consultation

- 8.6 The opinions and views of parents of children at the home are ascertained on a regular and frequent basis unless inappropriate, including views on:
    - Care at the home and the operation of the home
    - Adequacy of staff at any given time
    - Adequacy of space and furnishings in bedrooms
    - Privacy of facilities for washing, contacting significant people in the child's life and sense of personal space

- 8.7 Where consultation and involvement of a child's family is inappropriate, staff explain to the child why this is so and consult with significant others or an independent visitor, as appropriate.

- 8.8 Suitable means are frequently provided for any child with communication and/or learning difficulties to make her/his wishes and feelings known regarding care and treatment in the home, including availability of different adults who understand how the child communicates.

- 8.9 The way the home functions enhances every child's independence and opportunity to make everyday choices.

Standard 9: Privacy and Confidentiality [links to Reg. 15, ss. 22, 61, 64 CA 1989]

Outcome: Children's privacy is respected and information is confidentially handled.

- **9.1 The home and staff respect a child's wish for privacy and confidentiality as is consistent with good parenting and the need to protect the child.**

- The registered person provides procedural guidelines on privacy and confidentiality covering:
  - Access to case records by staff and others
  - Passing on information with child protection implications, and disclosure of illegal activities
  - Practical details about the way children's rooms are entered
  - Entry/interruptions without permission in emergencies or where children are considered at risk
  - Showering and bathing arrangements and use of toilets
  - Personal matters such as menstruation and washing clothes
  - Intimate personal care for disabled children, including administering medication and invasive clinical procedures where applicable

Standard 9: Privacy and Confidentiality

- 9.3 Staff know how to deal with, and share given information in confidence for child protection purposes.

- 9.4 Any restriction on communication by the child must have been agreed by the child's placing authority. If the child was not placed by a voluntary organisation or local authority, the child's parent or person with parental responsibility must agree to any restriction on communication by the child.

- 9.5 Siting of telephone/s and arrangements for payment are convenient, private and practical and accessible to disabled children if required. Arrangements regarding privacy and accessibility that differ from the above are agreed in placement plans and understood by the children.

- 9.6 Staff are sensitive to gender issues especially when dealing with children of the opposite sex.

- 9.7 Where the home accommodates children requiring staff help with intimate care or bodily functions or with lifting and handling, all staff involved must have received appropriate training and written guidelines on provision of such assistance, which are followed in practice. These guidelines cover boundaries to be observed and the requirements for the child concerned, where practicable, to be enable to express choices and to seek the child's consent regarding provision of her/his intimate care.

- 9.8 The registered persons provide guidance, for staff and children, on when it may be necessary to search a child's possessions. They are searched only in accordance with the guidance, and on clear grounds, explained to the child, and where failure to search would put at risk the welfare of the child/others. All searches are documented and signed by all present.

Standard 10: Provision and Preparation of Meals [links to Reg.13]

Outcome: Children enjoy healthy, nutritious meals that meet their dietary needs. They have opportunities to plan, shop for and prepare meals.

- **10.1 Children are provided with adequate quantities of suitably prepared food and drink having regard to their needs and wishes, and have the opportunity to shop for and prepare their own meals.**

- 10.2 Meals are set up to be well-managed, orderly, social occasions.

- 10.3 Children are provided with food in adequate quantities, properly prepared, wholesome and nutritious, with regard to their cultural, ethnic and religious backgrounds and dietary needs and choices (including the choice of vegetarian meals for children who wish it).

- 10.4 The record of menus (as served) demonstrates provision of a suitable and varied diet.

- 10.5 Medical advice is sought if children consistently refuse to eat and for those who over-eat or have other eating disorders.

- 10.6 Children are not routinely excluded from communal meals.

Standard 10: Provision and Preparation of Meals

- 10.7 Dining rooms and their furnishings are suitable for the number and needs of children and staff dining in them.

- 10.8 Children are able, with assistance where necessary, to prepare snacks and drinks for themselves at reasonable times.

- 10.9 Staff and children involved in preparing food for others have received appropriate training and/or are appropriately supervised in safe food handling and hygiene.

- 10.10 Meals (with drinks) are provided at reasonable set mealtimes, and food is either provided or readily available to children when they miss a set mealtime.

Standard 11: Personal Appearance, Clothing, Requisites & Pocket Money [links to Reg.14]

Outcome: Children are encouraged and enabled to choose their own clothes and personal requisites and have these needs fully met.

- **11.1 Children's clothing and personal requisite needs are fully met.**

- 11.2 Children are able to exercise choice in clothes and personal requisites they buy, through normal shopping arrangements. Younger children are accompanied by staff and older children given the choice of shopping alone subject to a risk assessment, or with staff.

- 11.3 Cultural, racial, ethnic or religious expectations regarding the choice of clothes or personal requisites are supported and positively promoted.

- 11.4 Children are able to keep their clothing and personal requisites/toiletries for their exclusive use, subject to risk assessments on particular items e.g. aerosols and razors.

- 11.5 Young women have their own supply of sanitary protection and do not have to request it from a central stock.

Standard 11: Personal Appearance

- 11.6 Staff provide, where appropriate, advice on the use of toiletries, cosmetics and sanitary protection.

- 11.7 Suitable and acceptable clothing and personal requisites are bought for any child who does not wish to, or is unable to, purchase her/his own.

- 11.8 Children's money is held in safe keeping and children sign the records. They are encouraged to manage their own finances through help with budgeting and banking.

- 11.9 There is a policy, implemented in practice and known to children, on personal allowances e.g. the purpose of different allowances, arrangements for receiving and reasons for withholding, monitoring of use and process for requests for special allowances are all clear.

Standard 12: Good Health and Well-Being [links to Reg.20]

Outcome: Children live in a healthy environment and their health needs are identified and services are provided to meet them, and their good health is promoted.

- **12.1 Physical, emotional and health needs of each child are identified and appropriate action taken to secure medical, dental and other health services needed to meet them. Each child is provided with guidance, advice and support on health and personal care issues appropriate to her/ his needs and wishes.**

- 12.2 Each child has a clear written health plan (within their placement plan) covering:

    - Medical history
    - Any specific medical or other health interventions which may be required
    - Any necessary preventive measures
    - Allergies or known adverse reactions to medication
    - Dental health needs
    - Any hearing needs
    - Any optical needs
    - Records of developmental checks
    - Specific treatment therapies or remedial

programmes needed in relation to physical, emotion or mental health
- Health monitoring required by staff
- The involvement of a child's parents or significant others in health issues.

■ 12.3 A written record is kept of all significant illnesses of, accidents by or injuries to children during their placement at the home.

■ 12.4 Each child is provided with guidance, advice and support, appropriate to her/his age, needs, culture and wishes, in relation to health and social issues including alcohol and illegal substance abuse, smoking, solvents, sex and relationship education, HIV infection, hepatitis and sexually transmitted diseases, and protecting oneself from prejudice, bullying and abuse, both within and outside the home.

■ 12.5 There is a policy and written guidance, implemented in practice, on promoting the health of children in the home including:

- Immunisation and screening
- Nutrition and diet
- Exercise and rest
- Personal hygiene
- Sexual health
- The effects of alcohol, smoking and other substances
- HIV and aids and other blood borne diseases

- 12.6 Children are actively discouraged from smoking, alcohol, illegal substance or solvent abuse and under-age sexual activity and given opportunities to discuss these issues openly and honestly with staff and peers.

- 12.7 Children, subject to age and understanding, can choose whether or not to be accompanied when being seen by a doctor, nurse or dentist, and, as far as is practicable, to see a doctor of either gender if they wish.

- 12.8 Children with particular health needs or a disability are provided with appropriate support and help. The registered person emphasises to staff the need to protect children's dignity at all times. The registered person ensures that any treatment which is prescribed or included in the child's placement plan or (where applicable) care plan is implemented taking the child's wishes into account.

- 12.9 Issues of personal hygiene are dealt with sensitively.

- 12.10 The needs of refugee children, asylum seekers and children from different racial and cultural backgrounds are understood by staff and specialist advice is sought where necessary.

Standard 13: Treatment and Administration of Medicines within the Home [links to Regs.20 & 21]

Outcome: Children's health needs are met and their welfare is safeguarded by the home's policies and procedures for administering medicines and providing treatment.

- **13.1 First aid, minor illness treatment and administration of medication given at the home (other than by a registered nurse, doctor or dentist) are given only by competent designated staff.**

- 13.2 A written record is kept by the home of all medication, treatment and first aid given to children, giving full reasons and medication/treatment which is signed by the responsible member of staff and is regularly monitored by a designated senior member of staff. A record is also kept of when and why prescribed medicines are not administered or are refused, when medication ceases and how and when medicines are disposed of.

- 13.3 When staff carry out skilled health tasks for children, these are carried out only on the written authorisation of the prescribing doctor or responsible nurse in relation to the individual child concerned, and by staff authorised by the prescribing doctor or a

Standard 13: Treatment and Administration of Medicines

nurse responsible for the tasks concerned. Records are kept of all such tasks carried out.

- 13.4 The registered person has obtained, and retains on file, prior written permission from a person with parental responsibility for each child, for the administration of first aid and appropriate non-prescription medication.

- 13.5 Staff are trained in the use of first aid and first aid boxes are provided within the home.

- 13.6 If a person is employed to work as a nurse at the home, that staff member holds a current registration as a nurse – confirmed by the registered person on their appointment that they are registered with the Nursing and Midwifery Council. The title of 'nurse' is not used by staff not so registered. If a person is employed as a nurse, that nurse should have access to a named senior nurse or doctor for professional guidance and consultation.

- 13.7 Children are given medication as prescribed for them; any refusal to take medication is recorded and, if frequent, reported to the prescribing practitioner.

- 13.8 Prescribed medication is only given to the child for whom it was prescribed, in accordance with prescription or pharmacy instructions and is not kept for general use or added to stock.

- 13.9 Children keeping and administering their own medication are assessed as being responsible to do so and are able to lock their medication somewhere not readily accessible to other children.

Standard 13: Treatment and Administration of Medicines

- 13.10 Prescribed and 'household' medication, other than that kept by individual children, is kept securely and there is a policy with written guidance, implemented in practice, for storing, disposing and administering medication.

- 13.11 The registered person has secured, and follows, qualified medical or nursing advice in a written protocol on the provision of non-prescription 'household' medicines to children.

Standard 14: Education [links to Reg.18]

Outcome: The education of children is actively promoted as valuable in itself and as part of their preparation for adulthood.

- **14.1 There is an education policy that shows how the home intends to promote and support educational attainment of children throughout the time they live there, including support by facilitating prompt arrival at school with the necessary equipment.**

- 14.2 Each child's file contains a copy of their Personal Education Plan (PEP) setting out a record of their educational achievements, needs and aspirations. Other relevant documents are kept on file including any record of educational history and any statement of special educational needs. Staff are familiar with these.

- 14.3 Each child is given full access to educational facilities, at both school level and in further or higher education as appropriate, wherever feasible and in line with the child's age, aptitude, needs, interests and potential.

- 14.4 The Personal Education Plan or placement plan explicitly address:

Standard 14: Education

- Education and whether the child's needs will be met by attending a particular educational establishment
- Any special educational needs/how they will be met
- The level of monitoring of a child's school attendance
- Parental/social worker involvement in the education of the child
- Dates of national exams such as SATS, GCSEs, AS and A levels and any others the child may take
- Staff with responsibility for liaising with schools, careers service etc.
- Arrangements for travelling to and from school

■ 14.5 Children are provided with facilities conducive to study/homework and are actively supported, including provision of books, computers and library membership, are helped with homework if they wish and participation in extra-curricular activities is not denied.

■ 14.6 In the absence of a child's parents, staff of the home attend parents' meeting and other school events.

■ 14.7 For children of compulsory school age not in school or a Pupil Referral Unit, the registered person has in place an educational programme during normal school hours: and works with the placing authority to secure appropriate full-time educational provision.

Standard 15: Leisure and Activities [links to Reg.18]

Outcome: Children are able to pursue their particular interests, develop confidence in their skills and are supported and encouraged by staff to engage in leisure activities.

- **15.1 There are ample opportunities for children to participate in a range of appropriate leisure activities, and the registered person allocates sufficient financial resources to fund leisure activities and trips.**

- 15.2 Children are encouraged to take part in activities and leisure interests which take account of their race, culture, language, religion, interests, abilities and disabilities.

- Birthdays, name days, cultural and religious festivals are celebrated where appropriate and children and staff plan events together. Support is available to enable disabled children to enjoy a range of activities both in and outside of the home.

- 15.3 Leisure interests and areas in which a child has talents or abilities are considered within the child's placement plan, and where applicable at care planning meetings and reviews. Consideration is given as to how they will be encouraged and financially supported.

Standard 15: Leisure and Activities

- 15.4 There is a proper balance between free and controlled time in the structure of the day. Activities reflect the choices of the children including doing nothing particular at times.

- 15.5 The safety of children is taken into account at all times and a recorded risk assessment made where substantial or unusual hazards are involved. Any high risk activity is supervised by persons holding the relevant qualification to supervise children's involvement in the activity concerned.

- 15.6 Children are encouraged to meet staff regularly to discuss the general running of the home, to plan activities and give their views. These views inform the choice of holidays, trips and outings. Staff engage with children in talking about and doing things and sharing their experiences.

- 15.7 Children have access to and a choice in the selection of, newspapers, books and magazines subject to their suitability. Children have access to suitable toys, music, books and games.

- 15.8 Consideration is given to individual circumstances of children in watching videos and television, and in using computer games and accessing the internet. Videos, games consoles and computer games may be watched/played only by children of the intended age range.

- No home shall have any videos or games certified 18. Systems and policies are in place to safeguard children when computer networking or on the

Standard 15: Leisure and Activities

internet and also to prevent the home from becoming dominated by use of computers and TV.

- 15.9 Trips out to events for enjoyment or interest are encouraged and/or organised by staff.

- 15.10 Children who wish to are helped to participate in the educational and leisure activities and facilities available to children in the home's locality.

- 15.11 Transport used by the home should be unmarked unless received as a donation carrying the charity's name. (this does not prevent schools which are children's homes from having the name of the school on the car/bus). The registered person checks all vehicles are taxed, MOTed, insured for purpose and well-maintained. Homes accommodating disabled children must have properly adapted vehicles.

- 15.12 Children are encouraged and enabled to make friendships with children of their own age outside the home. This may involve visiting each other's homes.

Standard 16: Complaints and Representation [links to Regs. 24 & 27]

Outcome: Any complaint will be addressed without delay and the complainant is kept informed of progress.

- **16.1 Children know how and feel able to complain if they are unhappy with any aspect of living in the home. Any complaint is addressed seriously and without delay, and a complaint will be fully responded to within a maximum of 28 days, and children are kept informed of the progress.**

- 16.2 Children, and where appropriate their families, significant others and independent visitors, are provided with information on how to complain, including how they can secure access to an advocate.

- 16.3 The home's complaints procedure:

    - Enables children, staff, family members and others involved with the children outside the home, to make both minor and major complaints
    - Precludes any person who is the subject of a formal complaint from taking any responsibility for the response to that complaint
    - Expressly forbids any reprisals against children or others making a complaint

Standard 16: Complaints and Representation

- Includes provision for both informal attempts at resolving the complaint and for the matter to be pursued further if the complainant is not satisfied with the proposed informal resolution
- Provides appropriately for the handling of complaints against the manager of the home
- Requires a written record to be made and kept of the person making the complaint including date, nature, action taken and outcome
- Does not restrict the issues they may complain about
- Provides for relevant issues to be referred promptly to other procedures, including the local social services authority where child protection issues are involved
- Provides appropriately for the handling of complaints against the registered person of the home
- Is accessible to disabled children in a suitable form
- Enables people other than the child to make with their consent, complaints on behalf of the child
- Provides for complainants to be kept inform of progress and to be provided with details of the outcome, in an accessible format, at the earliest opportunity

■ 16.4 There is a procedure for handling external complaints, e.g. from local shopkeepers, neighbours etc.

Standard 16: Complaints and Representation

- 16.5 The registered person has provided the home with a written policy and procedural guidelines on considering and responding to representations and complaints in accordance with legal requirements and relevant government guidance. The policy includes the right for all children placed by an authority to access the complaints procedure of that authority and details of how all complainants may contact CSCI.

- The policy is provided in suitable summary format/s to all parties concerned (any of whom are provided with a full procedure if requested).

- 16.6 All staff receive training in the complaints procedures covering the following areas:
    - What constitutes a complaint
    - What the procedure is for dealing with an informal complaint and how this is recorded
    - To whom a complaint is made outside the home
    - The procedure to be followed should a complaint not be resolved promptly by informal means
    - How the child can be assisted in making a complaint

- 16.7 The registered person of the home regularly reviews the records of complaints to check satisfactory operation of the complaints procedure, patterns of complaint and actions taken. The registered person takes any appropriate action from such a review.

Standard 17: Child Protection Procedures and Training [links to Reg.16]

Outcome: The welfare of children is promoted, children are protected from abuse, and an appropriate response is made to any allegation or suspicion of abuse.

- **17.1 There are systems in place to promote the safety and welfare of children and to ensure that children are protected from abuse, which are known and understood by all staff (including junior, ancillary, volunteer and agency staff).**

- 17.2 A copy of the local Area Child Protection Committee (LSCB) procedures is kept in the home. The registered person of the home ensures that staff have read these, understand and are knowledgeable about them.

- 17.3 There are clear procedures in line with the Children's Homes Regulations 2001 (known, understood and followed by all staff), for responding to allegations or suspicions of abuse, either by staff or by other children in the home, or by others, and that they include:

    - The requirement that staff who receive an allegation of abuse, or who suspect abuse, should avoid asking leading questions or giving inappropriate guarantees of confidentiality

- The requirement to report to the police any evidence of children becoming involved in prostitution, or of un-authorised persons picking children up, contacting children in the home or observed trying to make contact outside the home
- Instructions for staff on action to be taken if an allegation or suspicion of abuse becomes known to them involving the registered person or the person at the time in day to day charge of the home.

■ 17.4 The child protection procedures are consistent with the local policies and procedures agreed by the LSCB relevant to the area where the home is situated.

■ The child protection procedures have been submitted to the local LSCB, and comments taken into account.

■ 17.5 The registered person has liaised with the local Social Services Child Protection Co-ordinator or equivalent, to seek advice about local procedures and practice, and has discussed how the practices in the home relate to these. Any conflicts between locally agreed procedures and those of other placing authorities have also been discussed and resolved as far as possible.

■ 17.6 There is written guidance for staff which makes clear the ways in which the registered person of the home will ensure that members of staff subject to allegations against them will have access to information and support whilst an investigation ensues.

■ 17.7 Procedural guidance for staff clearly

Standard 17: Child Protection Procedures and Training

demonstrates the systems required in order to protect children and minimise the risk of abuse whilst the child is living in the home and includes guidance on:

- Making a full assessment of children's histories and any experience of abuse
- Observing contacts between children
- Supervision of children
- Supervision and support of staff
- Recognition of possible involvement of children in prostitution
- Confidentiality
- Physical contact between staff and children
- One to one time alone by staff with children
- Intimate care and invasive procedures
- Administering medication

■ 17.8 The registered person ensures provision of training for all staff, including ancillary and agency staff and volunteers, in the prevention and recognition of abuse (including in non-verbal children), dealing with disclosures or suspicions of abuse, and the home's child protection procedures. This training is included in induction programmes for new staff, including temporary or agency staff, and is ongoing for the staff group in keeping with aims and objectives of the home.

■ 17.9 The registered person and staff have routine links with other agencies concerned with child protection and do not work in isolation from them.

■ 17.10 The registered person follows any local

interagency protocols on prevention and
investigation of child prostitution.

Standard 18: Countering Bullying [links to Reg.16]

Outcome: Children are protected from bullying.

- **18.1 The registered person and staff create an atmosphere where bullying is known to be unacceptable. There is a policy on countering bullying, known to children and staff and effective in practice.**

- 18.2 The registered person has a policy on countering bullying which includes:
  - A definition of bullying, reviewed frequently with staff and children, which includes bullying by staff and bullying that may occur elsewhere than in the home and which covers different types of bullying
  - Measures to prevent bullying and respond to observed or reported bullying
  - Training for staff in awareness of, and effective strategies to counter, bullying.

- 18.3 This policy is available and known to all staff and children. The policy is implemented, and monitored for effectiveness in practice. Steps are taken to ensure that the policy is revised where necessary to ensure that staff reduce and respond to bullying effectively.

Standard 18: Countering Bullying

- 18.4 Children who are bullied are supported and children who may bully others given suitable guidance.

- 18.5 Registered person regularly carries out recorded risk assessments of times, places and circumstance in which risk of bullying is greatest, and takes action where feasible to reduce or counteract it.

Standard 19: Absence of a Child Without Authority [links to Regs. 16 & 30]

Outcome: Children who are absent without authority are protected in accordance with written guidance and responded to positively on return.

- **19.1 Children who are absent from the home without consent are protected in line with the home's written policy and guidance.**

- 19.2 The written procedures of the home identifying action to be taken when a child is absent without authority cover the following areas:

  - Searching for any child missing or believed to have run away from the home
  - Reporting missing children to the police, to the child's placing authority and to others (including parents), subject to consultation with placing authority
  - Action to obtain information about the whereabouts of a missing child and to try to ensure the safety and welfare of that child
  - The collection and return of missing children when found
  - Action to be taken on the child's return
  - Allowing for any individual arrangements based on a child's needs as agreed in his/her placement plan

Standard 19: Absence of a Child Without Authority

- 19.3 The procedure specifically addresses action to be taken in the event of the absence of a child looked after in taking into account different legal statuses e.g. voluntarily accommodated or a care order.

- 19.4 On return to the home, the child is seen if possible by her/his social worker or a person independent of the home to consider the reasons for the absence. Where this is not possible, the reasons are recorded and agreed with the placing authority. Any reasons given for being absent are considered in relation to how the child is cared for and the child's placement plan.

- 19.5 Any report from a child that s/he went missing because of abuse at the home is referred immediately to the local social services for consideration under LSCB procedures and appropriate protective action taken.

- 19.6 Written records are made of the circumstances of all incidents of absconding, all action taken by staff, the circumstances of the child's return, reasons given for absconding and actions taken in response.

- 19.7 All staff are aware of, and do not exceed, the measures allowed under current law and government guidance to prevent a child leaving without permission.

- 19.8 When a child is considered likely to go missing, the registered person has agreed procedures to monitor her/him and to specify how s/he may be prevented from leaving. Procedures may include physical modification to premises, behavioural and/or therapeutic approaches to change behaviour, or agreed physical restraint. Any such measures must be used as agreed in the child's placement plan and (where applicable) care plan.

- 19.9 The registered person maintains regular contact with schools to monitor attendance. Where children are thought to be especially vulnerable/prone to frequent absences, this involves daily contact with school. Where there is continued absence or a worrying pattern of absence from school, the registered person initiates a review of placement plan, (where applicable) care plan and of relevant current care practice of the home.

Standard 20: Notification of Significant Events [links to Reg.30]

Outcome: All significant events relating to the protection of children accommodated in the home are notified by the registered person of the home to the appropriate authorities.

- **20.1 The registered person has a system in place to notify within 24 hours persons and appropriate authorities of occurrence of significant events in accordance with Regulation 30.**

- 20.2 The registered person ensures notification to parents concerned of any other significant incident affecting their child's welfare, unless not reasonably practicable, or likely to place the child's welfare at risk.

- 20.3 A written record is kept including details of action taken, and outcome of any action/investigation, following notifiable events.

- 20.4 The registered person has a system for notification to placing authorities of any serious concerns about emotional/mental health of child such that assessment under the Mental Health Act 1983 would be requested.

- 20.5 The registered person requests a meeting to discuss proposed action following any incident notified under Regulation 30 or any initial steps taken to deal with any emergency (where a meeting is not held, this is with the agreement of the placing authority).

Standard 21: Relationship with Children [links to Reg.17]

Outcome: Children enjoy sound relationships with staff based on honesty and mutual respect.

- **21.1 Relationships between staff and children are based on mutual respect and understanding and clear professional and personal boundaries which are effective for both individuals and the group.**

- 21.2 Staff employed at the home are able to set and maintain safe, consistent and understandable boundaries for the children in relation to acceptable behaviour.

- 21.3 Expectation of behaviour for both staff and children are clearly understood and negotiated by those living and working at the home, including exercising appropriate control over children in the interests of their own welfare and the protection of others.

- 21.4 In day to day decision making, staff demonstrate an appropriate balance between:
  - Each child's wishes and preferences
  - The needs of individual children
  - The needs of the present resident group
  - The protection of others (including the public) from harm/

Standard 21: Relationship with Children

- 21.5 All staff receive training in positive care/control, communication between staff and children is generally positive and disagreements dealt with reasonably.

- 21.6 Children are looked after without favouritism or antipathy toward individual or group within the home.

- 21.7 Deployment of staff facilitates continuity of staff providing care to individual children. Where children require personal care, their choices of which staff provide that care are maximised.

Standard 22: Behaviour Management [links to Reg. 17]

Outcome: Children assisted to develop socially acceptable behaviour through encouragement of acceptable behaviour and constructive staff response to inappropriate behaviour.

- **22.1 Staff respond positively to acceptable behaviour, and where the behaviour of children is regarded as unacceptable by staff, it is responded to by constructive, acceptable and known disciplinary measures approved by the registered person.**

- 22.2 The registered person has a clear written policy, procedures and guidance for staff based on a code of conduct setting out control, disciplinary and restraint measures permitted and emphasising need to reinforce positive messages to children for the achievement of acceptable behaviour.

- 22.3 Control and disciplinary measures are based on establishing positive relationships with children which are designed to help the child. Such measures are fairly and consistently applied. They also encourage reparation and restitution and reduce the likelihood of negative behaviour becoming the focus.

- 22.4 The consequences of unacceptable behaviour are clear to staff and children and any measures applied are relevant to the incident.

Standard 22: Behaviour Management

- 22.5 Any measures taken to respond to unacceptable behaviour are appropriate to the age, understanding and individual needs of the child e.g. taking into account that unacceptable or challenging behaviour may be the result of illness, bullying, certain disabilities such as autism or communication difficulties.

- 22.6 Sanctions and physical restraint are not excessive or unreasonable.

- 22.7 Physical restraint is only used to prevent likely injury to the child concerned or to others, or likely serious damage to property. Restraint is not used as a punishment, as a means to enforce compliance with instructions, or in response to challenging behaviour which does not give rise to reasonable expectation of injury to someone or serious damage to property.

  NB. For schools which are children's homes, this does not prevent the use of restraint in those circumstances permitted by s.550A Education Act 1996.

- 22.8 The registered person's policy on the use and techniques of physical restraint and other forms of physical intervention, and the circumstances in which they may be used, is consistent with any relevant government guidance. All staff of the home are aware of and follow the registered person's policy. Training covers reducing or avoiding the need to use physical restraint. All staff have signed a copy of the policy and evidence of this is retained on their personnel file.

Standard 22: Behaviour Management

- 22.9 A record of the use of restraint is kept in a separate dedicated bound and numbered book, and includes name of child, date, time and location, details of behaviour requiring restraint, details of restraint including name/s of staff and others present and effectiveness and consequences including any injury caused. The signature of the person authorised by the registered person to make this record is also required.

- 22.10 A similar and separate record of any sanctions will also be kept in the same way.

- 22.11 The registered person will regularly monitor record books to ensure compliance with the home's policy, procedure and guidance and to identify any patterns to incidents. The registered person records any comment on the appropriateness of individual uses of sanctions or use of restraint, together with any subsequent action taken, and signs against each entry to confirm the monitoring has taken place.

- 22.12 Measures of control, discipline and restraint used by the home are made clear to placing authority, child, parent/s or carers before or, in an emergency placement, at the time child is to move into the home.

- 22.13 Children are encouraged to develop a proper awareness of their rights and responsibilities. Staff and children alike are clear that each individual has rights and responsibilities in relation to those who live and work in the home and people in the

Standard 22: Behaviour Management

community. Where there has been physical intervention, the child will have the right to be examined by a registered nurse or GP within 24 hours.

- 22.14 All children are given an opportunity to discuss incidents individually or in a regular forum where unsafe behaviour can be discussed by them and adults. When disciplinary measures or restraint are used, children are encouraged to write or have their views recorded, signed and if possible kept by the home.

- 22.15 Unless the registered person can demonstrate that this is not appropriate, the home has procedures and guidance on police involvement in the home, which have been agreed with the local police and about which staff are clear.

- 22.16 Staff meetings address issues of control and agree practicable and acceptable means of responding to behaviour and control problems.

Standard 23: Location, Design and Size of the Home [links to Reg.31]

Outcome: Children live in well designed and pleasant homes providing sufficient space to meet their needs.

- **23.1 Home's location, design and size are in keeping with its purpose and function. It serves the needs of the children it accommodates and provides an environment supportive to each child's development.**

- 23.2 The home is located to take account of transport, education, health, leisure and employment facilities.

- 23.3 Where the home accommodates disabled children, suitable aids and adaptations and any special furniture or equipment required are provided and particular attention is paid to the following:

  - Accommodation ensures that disabled children have equal access to all parts of the building
  - Handrails or other mobility aids appropriately sited
  - Lifts and stairs are adapted and safe for all users
  - If children have visual impairments, colours and lighting are appropriately chosen
  - If children have hearing impairments, an induction loop system, telephone and television adaptations and noise insulation are provided
  - Safe storage of equipment and wheelchairs, with proper arrangements for recharging batteries

Standard 23: Location, Design and Size of the Home

- 23.4 Where a home accommodates disabled children an occupational therapist has assessed the premises and her/his recommendations have been adopted.

- 23.5 Physical restrictions on normal movement within the home are used only in relation to a child where the restriction has been agreed in her/his placement plan (and care plan if appropriate) and are used only where necessary to safeguard and promote that child's welfare. Such restrictions for one child do not impose similar restrictions on other children.

- 23.6 There are no outstanding requirements or recommendations relating to the home from:
  - Planning authority
  - Building control authority
  - Fire service
  - Environmental health authority
  - DfES or OfSTED

- 23.7 The design, layout and use of the accommodation are such that children's individual care and privacy are not compromised.

- 23.8 The home's premises are not used for functions unrelated to the home which compromise or have an adverse effect on the care of children in the home.

- 23.9 Effective precautions, acceptable to all, are taken to ensure the security of the home from access by unauthorised persons.

- 23.10 The registered person maintains appropriate links with the local community to the home and, where appropriate, promotes positive links.

Standard 24: Accommodation
[links to Regs. 15 & 31]

Outcome: Children enjoy homely accommodation, decorated, furnished and maintained to a high standard, providing adequate facilities for their use.

- **24.1 Home provides adequate good quality domestic style facilities for those living on the premises consistent with the purpose and function of the home, and is maintained in good order throughout.**

- 24.2 Home is decorated and furnished to a standard which creates a pleasant domestic environment, appropriate to number, gender mix, disability, age, culture and ethnic background of those accommodated.

- 24.3 The interior and exterior of the home are maintained in a good state of structural and decorative repair. There is a satisfactory maintenance and prepare programme and any damage is repaired promptly. Gardens and/or hard play areas are safe and well maintained. The home is kept clean.

- 24.4 There is a distinction between private and community shared space. Where a school is a children's home, there is a clear separation between residential and non-residential buildings.

- 24.5 Each child has a single bedroom or her/his own area in a double bedroom, of a suitable size with bed

Standard 24: Accommodation

and bedding, seating, storage for clothes, lockable or otherwise safe storage for personal possessions, a window with curtains, lighting sufficient to read by, carpet or other appropriate floor covering and heating.

- 24.6 In a school which is a home, as far as possible children are given the option of a single room. From April 2003, there are no more than 4 children in a bedroom and at no time are there odd sharing a bedroom. Bunk beds are not used for children aged 13 or over unless they request it, and are not used for children for whom there would be a safety risk. Where bunk beds are used, there has to be the floor space comparable to their being 2 separate beds in the room. Any request by a child to change bedroom is given urgent consideration and agreed if feasible.

- 24.7 The registered person takes into account the potential for abusive behaviour before agreeing to the sharing of bedrooms.

- 24.8 Where necessary because of children's disabilities or other needs, an effective emergency call system is provided for summoning prompt staff assistance.

- 24.9 Where needed by children, the home provides sufficient, regularly serviced appropriate equipment such as lifts, hoists etc. Rooms used to accommodate disabled children must, if relevant, have sufficient space for the easy manoeuvrability of wheelchairs, hoists etc.

Standard 24: Accommodation

- 24.10 Children are able and encouraged to personalise their bedrooms.

- 24.11 1 or more telephones are provided for the exclusive use of children in the home. These offer acceptable levels of privacy for personal calls and are kept in working order. Disabled children are enabled to use the telephone in private as far as possible.

- 24.12 Facilities for children to study are quiet, with sufficient seating, desk/table space, lighting, storage for books and study materials and are available when needed.

- 24.13 There are facilities for children to pursue personal hobbies at the home, with sufficient and secure storage for safekeeping of materials.

- 24.14 Children are given opportunities to have a say in general décor, furnishings and upkeep of the home if they wish.

- 24.15 There are rooms in which children can meet privately with visitors and space for private activities, play and recreation.

- 24.16 Staff sleep-in rooms are not part of the communal living area, are located close to children's bedrooms to respond to night time needs. Where more than one staff member sleeps in on the same night, there are separate sleeping-in rooms.

- 24.17 A home that provides temporary accommodation as detailed in its Statement of Purpose may, under certain circumstances, be

Standard 24: Accommodation

exempted from the requirement to provide each child with a single bedroom or her/his own area in a double bedroom, provided a risk assessment has been undertaken, and welfare needs of children are not compromised.

- 24.18 In any home not also a school, children share bedrooms only where they have agreed this. Children accommodated in emergency provision are not placed in a shared bedroom (other than with siblings) until an assessment has been carried out.

- 24.19 Where they are relevant, schools which are children's homes meet the requirements of the School Premises Regulations 1999.

Standard 25: Bathrooms and Washing Facilities [links to Reg.31]

Outcome: Children's privacy is respected when washing.

- **25.1 Baths, showers and toilets are of a number and standard to meet the needs of the children.**

- 25.2 there is at least 1 toilet for every 4 children accommodated, with nearby hand washing and drying provision. A toilet that is in a bathroom or shower room is not the only toilet in the home.

- 25.3 Subject to standard 25.9, both baths and showers are available for children's use and there is a minimum of 1 bath or shower for every 5 children accommodated.

- 25.4 Bathrooms, showers and toilets are sited and designed to take account of the children's needs for privacy, dignity, safety and any disability, and readily accessible from sleeping and recreational areas of the home. Showers which are not in individual rooms are provided in individual cubicles or fully individually curtained for privacy.

- 25.5 Bathrooms and toilets are accessible to disabled children in accordance with the home's Statement of Purpose. Those requiring it, have personal assistance provided so as to maximise privacy and dignity.

Standard 25: Bathrooms and Washing Facilities

- 25.6 Staff (not children) are able, in an emergency to open doors to bathrooms/showers/toilets from the outside.

- 25.7 In homes accommodating more than 5 children, staff use separate toilet/bathroom/showers. In homes accommodating 5 or fewer children, staff may use the same facilities but there is a clear understanding they may not use them when children are present.

- 25.8 Hot water accessible to children under 8, or children with disabilities which place them at risk from excessively hot water, is maintained at no more than 43°C at taps and other outlets accessible to them.

- 25.9 The above standards apply to schools which are children's homes except that:

    - In boys' residential units, urinals may be provided instead of no more than two thirds of the required number of toilets.
    - There should be a minimum of 1 bath or shower for every 7 children accommodated, but a higher ratio when required by children's' needs.

    NB. This standard is subject to the requirements of the School Premises Regulations 1999 where applicable.

Standard 26: Health, Safety and Security [links to Regs. 22, 23, 31 & 32]

Outcome: Children live in homes that provide physical safety and security.

- **26.1 Positive steps are taken to keep children, staff and visitors safe from risk of fire and other hazards.**

- 26.2 Risk assessments are carried out, recorded and regularly reviewed. Such assessments are carried out for premises/grounds, children's known and likely activities (permitted and illicit), potential for bullying and abuse in or out of the home, and where applicable the impact of emergency admissions for admitted child and existing group.

- 26.3 The registered person of the home regularly reviews the implementation and effectiveness of action identified as a result of risk assessments carried out.

- 26.4 Registered person has planned responses to a range of foreseeable crises, and major incidents or crises since last inspection satisfactorily managed.

- Gas installations/boilers are inspected at least annually and electrical installations/equipment checked at least every 3 years. Environmental Health Services have assessed food storage and preparation

Standard 26: Health, Safety and Security

provision and any recommendations are implemented within the time-scale advised.

- 26.7 Children and staff know the emergency fire evacuation procedures, including those for use at night.

- 26.8 The registered person implements requirements of the local fire authority, to the time-scales agreed. Subject to any local arrangements agreed:

  - At least 4 fire drills, including evacuation of staff and children from building and drills held at night, take place in a 12 month period, and are recorded
  - Regular testing of emergency lighting, fire alarms and fire fighting equipment
  - Any deficiency identified from drills, tests or visits from fire safety officer noted, and action
  - Local fire authority consulted about fire precaution measures, and is consulted further if any significant extension, change of use or alteration made to premises

- 26.9 The registered person ensures that the home has current public and employee liability insurance (minimum value £5M). Certificates of insurance specify the name and address of a particular home.

- 26.10 Where the home uses medical devices and equipment, or equipment for disabled children e.g. hoists, lifts, wheelchairs, it has arrangements to receive and respond to relevant hazard and other warning notices from the Medical Devices Agency.

- 26.11 The location and design of car access and parking areas at the home minimise risk to children.

Standard 27: Vetting of Staff and Visitors [links to Reg. 16, 26 & 27]

Outcome: Careful selection and vetting of all staff and volunteers working with children in the home and monitoring of visitors to prevent exposure to potential abusers.

- **27.1 There is a written record of the recruitment process which is followed in respect of all staff (including ancillary staff and those on a contractual/ sessional basis) and volunteers who work with children in the home, including evidence that all requirements of Schedule 2 of Children's Homes Regulations 2001 have been met in every case.**

- 27.2 The registered person's system for recruiting staff and volunteers to work with children in the home includes effective system to decide on appointment, or refusal of appointment, in the light of any criminal convictions or other concerns about suitability that are declared or discovered through the recruitment process.

- 27.3 Registered person ensures any agency staff who work with children in the home have successfully passed Children's Homes Regulations checks within previous 12 months. There must be evidence of this, which is placed on their file.

Standard 27: Vetting of Staff and Visitors

- The check will be at 'enhanced' level for staff and volunteers involved in regularly caring for, supervising, training or being in sole charge of children, and at the 'standard' level for all others working as paid staff or volunteers.

- 27.4 The registered person has taken reasonably practicable steps to ensure that where children are driven in taxis arranged by the home, they are either accompanied by staff or other arrangements have been made to ensure their welfare.

- 27.5 Staff members and others subject to the above checks do not normally start work at the home until all checks required are completed. Exceptionally, a member of staff may be allowed to do so while the outcome of some checks is awaited. In every case, the appropriate check via the CRB must have been completed before the person starts work. In such circumstances, the registered person must ensure that:

    - The individual is directly supervised at all times at a level that prevents them having unsupervised contact with children in the home
    - Such circumstances are exceptional
    - The registered person has taken all reasonable steps to complete the recruitment process and to 'chase' outstanding information, and
    - The registered person has taken all reasonable steps to avoid such circumstances occurring.

Standard 27: Vetting of Staff and Visitors

- Continued employment, in such circumstances, is subject to satisfactory outcomes from the checks.

- 27.6 The registered person provides information about the purpose of the home, consistent with its Statement of Purpose, to all applicants for all posts in the home.

- 27.7 Wherever practicable, short-listed applicants for appointments to any post are invited to meet staff and children (subject to children's agreement) prior to an appointment decision and their observations sought which are taken into account in the appointment decision. In such circumstances, candidates are not given unsupervised access to children.

- 27.8 Any employment references provided by the registered person on any existing or past staff member for work with children clearly state if there are any concerns regarding suitability to work with children.

- 27.9 Adults living in household on premises of the home who are not members of staff are checked through the CRB at the 'standard' level of checking.

- 27.10 Any visitor to the home who has not been satisfactorily checked through CRB, is not allowed unsupervised access to the home.

- 27.11 There is a clear policy, with procedures, implemented in practice, for monitoring such people. There is a system in place to record all visits made to the home.

Standard 27: Vetting of Staff and Visitors

- Children are given clear written and verbal guidance on arrangements for receiving their own visitors. Visiting parents and relatives are not given unsupervised access to other children in the home.

Standard 28: Staff Support
[links to Reg.27]

Outcome: Children are looked after by staff who are themselves supported and guided in safeguarding and promoting the children's welfare.

- **28.1 All staff, including domestic staff and the registered person of the home, are properly managed, supported and understand to whom they are accountable.**

- 28.2 All staff and others working in the home received at least 1.5 hours of 1:1 supervision from a senior member of staff each month.

- New staff receive 1:1 supervision at least fortnightly during the first 6 months of employment.

- Agency staff and those employed infrequently to cover staff absences must receive 1:1 supervision no less frequently than after each 8 shifts worked in the home.

    NB. In schools that are homes, staff receive at 1.5 hours one to one supervision from a senior member of staff each half-term. New staff receive 1:1 supervision at least fortnightly during the first 2 terms of their employment.

    Agency staff and those employed infrequently must receive 1:1 supervision no less than once every half term they work more than 10 shifts or days at school.

Standard 28: Staff Support

- Records are kept of agreed action following all supervision meetings.

- 28.3 Written record kept in home detailing time, date and length of each supervision, signed by supervisor and member of staff at end of session and is available for CSCI inspection.

- 28.4 Supervision of individual staff working with children addresses the following issues:

  - Responses to and methods of working with children
  - Work with any child for whom s/he is key worker
  - The staff member's role, including accountability, in fulfilling the home's statement of purpose
  - The staff member's work in fulfilling the placement plan for individual children
  - Degree of personal involvement, feelings, concerns and stress
  - Staff development and training
  - Feedback on performance
  - Guidance on current and new tasks, including the setting and maintenance of standards
  - Personal issues which may impinge her/his ability to carry out duties effectively

- 28.5 Suitable arrangements exist for professional supervision of the registered person of the home.

- 28.6 All staff, including the registered person, have received written job descriptions and person specifications stating clearly their responsibilities, duties currently expected of them and their line of

Standard 28: Staff Support

accountability. Job descriptions are subject to periodic review.

- 28.7 All staff have their performance individually and formally appraised at least annually by their line manager. The employee's personnel file contains a record of the appraisal.

- 28.8 Staff are provided with written guidance on the home's procedures and practice. This is kept up to date, is accessible, and where applicable is available on the policy areas detailed in appendix 1. Staff are informed of the home's complaints procedure.

- 28.9 Staff of the home have access to sources of advice and counselling.

- 28.10 Staff meetings occur at least monthly. Meetings have an agenda and are minuted.

Standard 29: Overall Competence of Staff [links to Regs. 25, 26 & 27]

Outcome: Children receive the care and services they need from competent staff.

- **29.1 The overall competence of staff, both as a staff group and on individual shifts, is satisfactory in relation to the fulfilment of the home's Statement of Purpose, the care plans, placement plans and needs (including any nursing needs) of individual children in the home, the number and mix of children in the home, and any particular difficulties being experienced by the home.**

- 29.2 There are clear arrangements for staff to deputise in the registered person's absence, and the deputy to the registered person of the home has at least 1 year's relevant supervisory experience.

- 29.3 Staff members who are placed in charge of the home and other staff at particular times have substantial relevant experience of working in the home, are not themselves temporary staff, and have successfully completed their induction and probationary periods.

- 29.4 By January 2004, all care staff are at least 18 years old, those given sole responsibility for children or a management role at least 21 (and no person

Standard 29: Overall Competence of Staff

works in a children's home unless they are at least 4 years older than the oldest child accommodated).

- 29.5 A minimum ratio of 80% of all care staff have completed their Level 3 in the Caring for Children and Young People NVQ by January 2005.

- Staff may hold other qualifications that require similar competencies, and these may be courses developed locally which are accredited.

- New staff engaged from January 2004 need to hold the Caring for Children and Young People NVQ or other qualification which matches the competencies or begin working towards them within 3 months of joining the home.

  NB. If the above standard is not met, guidance on how this may be responded to by inspectors is provided by CSCI via www.csci.org.uk

- 29.6 Staff rotas have time scheduled to ensure that hand-over sessions, spending time with individual children, completion of records, planning and carrying out of care programmes occur with compromising overall care of children.

- 29.7 Children are not given responsibility over other children, nor given responsibilities to compensate for any lack of staff in the home.

- Children who are given responsibility for specific tasks are sufficiently supervised by staff to ensure that they fulfil their roles appropriately.

Standard 29: Overall Competence of Staff

- 29.8 The registered person has in place a staff disciplinary procedure which is clear that a member of staff may be sent home, as a neutral act, pending consideration of, or completion of an investigation of, any suspicion or allegation of abuse or serious concern.

- The procedure clearly separates staff disciplinary processes from child protection enquiries and criminal proceedings, and is known by staff.

Standard 30: Sufficient Numbers of Staff [links to Reg. 25]

Outcome: Staff are sufficient in number, experience and qualification to meet the needs of the children.

- **30.1 The home is staffed at all times of day and night, at or above the minimum level specified under standard 30.2. Records of staff actually working in the home demonstrate achievement of this level.**

- 30.2 Registered person's staffing policy ensures staffing is adequate to meet the homes Statement of Purpose. The home's staffing is sufficient in practice to meet the needs of the children accommodated. The staffing policy is set out in the Statement of Purpose and states:

  - Number of care staff required to be on duty by day
  - Number of care staff required to be on duty by night, and whether required to be waking or sleeping in
  - Number of ancillary staff required to be on duty in addition to care staff at defined times of day or night
  - Agreed start and finishing times for night staffing
  - Arrangements for managing the staff on duty group by day and night

Standard 30: Sufficient Numbers of Staff

- Minimum number of staff to be present in the building during the day
- Arrangements for calling senior staff support if required

- 30.3 The registered person makes every effort to achieve continuity of staffing such that children's attachments are not overly disrupted.

- No more than half the staff on duty at any one time day or night are to be from an external agency, and no member of staff from an external agency is to be alone on duty at night in the home.

- 30.4 The registered person increases the number of staff above the minimum required by the Statement of Purpose where children's needs, numbers, or other circumstances require this in order to safeguard and promote the welfare of each individual child.

- 30.5 Where only one member of staff is on duty at any time, a risk assessment has been carried out and recorded in writing, and this has demonstrated that there is no unacceptable level of risk from such an arrangement.

- 30.6 Children always have a member of staff responsible for them. They know who that member of staff is and how to contact them.

- There is at least one member of staff responsible for each identifiable group of children, within or outside the home, with the means to call for immediate back up from at least one other member of staff if necessary.

Standard 30: Sufficient Numbers of Staff

- 30.7 Staffing arrangements for staff sickness and absence enable the home's staffing policy to be maintained.

- 30.8 The staff group in day to day contact with children includes staff of both genders whenever possible. Where the home's Statement of Purpose makes it explicit that the home uses staff of one gender only, clear guidance is provided and implemented on how children are enabled to maintain relationships with members of the opposite gender to the staff group. Staffing arrangements also take into consideration children's ethnic and cultural backgrounds and any disabilities they may have.

- 30.9 Staff know which children and adults are sleeping in the house each night.

Standard 31: Training & Development [links to Reg.27]

Outcome: Children are looked after by staff who are trained and competent to meet their needs.

- **31.1 Staff receive training and development opportunities that equip them with the skills required to meet the needs of the children and the purpose of the home.**

- 31.2 The registered person has an induction training programme for all newly appointed care and ancillary staff (including any agency, temporary, volunteer and student staff) which includes guidance on child protection.

- New staff are supervised, and are clear about accountability and reporting lines and procedures with regard to emergencies, health and safety, child protection and notification of incidents.

- 31.3 An introduction to child protection procedures, fire training, medical procedures and recording is provided for all staff before they start work.

- All care staff receive their full induction with 6 weeks of joining and their foundation training within six months. Both induction and foundation training are to the National Training Organisation's specification.

- 31.4 All child care staff have a personal development plan, and receive at least 6 paid days of training a

Standard 31: Training & Development

year. They have, where appropriate, access to continuing and post qualifying training in child care.

- A written record of all training for all staff is maintained in the home.

- 31.5 Where staff members do not already have the necessary skills, they have been provided with access to programmes of training available which address the issues detailed in appendix 2.

- 31.6 Staff do not smoke with or in the presence of children accommodated in the home. Only in exceptional circumstances and with the registered person's express permission do staff have a small alcoholic drink whilst on duty e.g. Christmas lunch.

- Under no circumstances does a member of staff use any illegal drug or other substance in the home or take any such substance into the home.

- In homes accommodating disabled children who need to be lifted or handled, staff are trained in lifting and handling techniques.

Standard 32: Monitoring by the Person Carrying on the Home [links to Reg.33]

Outcome: The person carrying on the home monitors the welfare of the children in the home.

- **32.1 Where the person carrying on the home does not manage the home on a day-to-day basis, s/he must visit the home at least once a month in accordance with the regulations. After the visit, and within 2 weeks, s/he should complete a written report on the conduct of the home. A copy of the report is sent to the CSCI and a copy is lodged in the home for the manager and staff to read and respond to.**

- 32.2 Visits are generally carried out unannounced. They include checks on the home's daily log, records of complaints, disciplinary measures and use of restraint, assessment of the physical condition of the building, furniture and equipment of the home, and provide an opportunity for any child or member of staff who wishes to meet the visitor (in private if they wish).

- 32.3 Action is taken by the registered person on recommendations or issues of concern raised in such reports.

Standard 33: Monitoring of the Operation of the Home [links to Reg.34]

Outcome: The care of children accommodated in the home is monitored and continually adapted in the light of information about how it is operating.

- 33.1 There are systems in place to monitor the performance of the home against its Statement of Purpose, and for regular reviewing of the Statement, and the registered provider ensures that performance is monitored in accordance with the Children's Homes Regulations 2001.

- The registered person of the home monitors and signs the home's records at least once a month, to identify any patterns or issues requiring action. S/he takes action to improve or adjust provisions where necessary.

- 33.2 Action is taken if necessary in relation to any concentration, trend or pattern in recorded issues or events to improve the safeguarding and promotion of the welfare of children and quality of care in the home.

- 33.3 The registered person considers the reasons for any high incidence of police involvement with children from the home, high proportion of children not at school, suspended or excluded, or high staff

Standard 33: Monitoring of the Operation of the Home

turnover. Any consequential action necessary is carried out.

- 33.4 The registered person can demonstrate the home is operating in accordance with its Statement of Purpose.

- 33.5 The registered person has a written development plan, reviewed annually, for the future of the home.

- 33.6 Copies of inspection reports by the CSCI are prominently displayed within the home and made available to all staff, children, parents and on request to placing authorities of existing children or considering placing a child.

Standard 34: Business Management [links to Regs. 8 & 36]

Outcome: Children enjoy the stability of efficiently run homes.

- **34.1 Administration of the home is efficient and the home is financially sound.**

- 34.2 The registered person has the necessary ability to plan, budget and administer the finances for the home to ensure that it is run on a sound financial basis.

- 34.3 The registered person of the home has:

  - By January 2005, a professional qualification relevant to working with children – either NVQ level 4 or the Dip.S.W. (or other qualification that matches the competencies required by that NVQ)
  - By January 2005, a qualification at level 4 NVQ in management (or another qualification that matches the competencies required by that NVQ)
  - At least 2 years' experience of working with children within the past 5 years and
  - In addition at least 1 year's experience of working at a senior level in a residential setting

  NB. If the above standard is not met, guidance on how this may be responded to by inspectors is provided by CSCI at www.csci.org.uk

Standard 34: Business Management

- 34.4 The job description of the registered manager clearly states in writing the responsibilities and duties and the person to whom s/he is accountable and any change in the person to whom s/he is accountable has been notified in writing to the registered manager.

- 34.5 For the transitional period referred to in 34.3, newly appointed managers without appropriate qualifications, must begin training within 3 months.

- 34.6 The registered manager of the home exercises effective leadership of the home's staff and operation, such that the home delivers the best possible child care.

- 34.7 Funding of the home is sufficient to finance fulfilment of the Statement of Purpose, national minimum standards, and any registration conditions.

- 34.8 Accounts demonstrate the home is financially viable and likely to have sufficient funding to continue to fulfil its Statement of Purpose for the next 12 months.

- 34.9 The registered manager takes reasonable steps to ensure good relationships with neighbours and the wider community.

- 34.10 Where a residential special school is a children's home and the head of school is the registered manager, it is the head of care (or equivalent post-holder) who meets the qualification requirements set out in 34.3. The head of care should not also be the head of school.

Standard 35: Children's Individual Case Files [links to Reg. 28]

Outcome: Children's needs, development and progress are recorded to reflect their individuality.

- **35.1 Each child has a permanent private and secure record of their history and progress which can, in compliance with legal requirements, be seen by the child and by the child's parents as appropriate.**

- 35.2 Each child's file contains information detailed in Sch.3 Children's Homes Regulations, and each child made aware s/he may read files (except confidential or third party information), is actively encouraged to do so, correct errors and add personal statements.

Standard 36: Secure Accommodation and Refuges [links to Reg.11, ss.22, 61, 64 CA 1989]

Outcome: Children living in secure units or refuges receive the same measures to safeguard and promote their welfare as they should in other children's homes.

- **36.1 Apart from measures necessary to the home's status as a secure unit or refuge, children resident in secure units or refuges receive the same care services as they should in other children's homes.**

- 36.2 Children in secure accommodation within a home are cared for consistently with these national minimum standards, with only those adaptations essential in the home concerned for maintenance of security.

- 36.3 Children in homes which are refuges approved under the Children Act 1989 are looked after in accordance with these national minimum standards, with only those adaptations essential in the home concerned as a result of its status as a refuge.

Appendices

Appendix 1: Policy Issues for Inclusion in Staff Guidance

1. Admission and reception of children
2. Methods of care and control
3. Health policy
4. Education policy
5. Permissible sanctions
6. Use of restraint
7. Case recording and access to records
8. Care and placement plans
9. Use of each child's placement plan
10. Countering bullying
11. Log book and diary recording
12. Confidentiality
13. Administration of finance (petty cash) and security
14. Repairs and maintenance
15. Fire precautions and emergency procedures
16. Countering risks identified through the home's risk assessments extending to which all or part of premises may be locked as a security measure

Appendix 1: Policy Issues for Inclusion in Staff Guidance

17. The health and safety policy (including food hygiene)
18. Policy on room searches
19. Child protection
20. Arrangements for regulating and vetting visitors
21. HIV/aids awareness, confidentiality and infection control
22. Responding to allegations or suspicions of abuse
23. Treatment of children who have been abused
24. Rostering shift hand-overs
25. Staffing policy
26. Sleeping-in, bed-time and night supervision
27. Physical contact with children
28. Spending 1:1 time alone with children
29. Care practices towards children of the opposite sex
30. The particular care needs of children from minority ethnic groups
31. Practices within the home to combat racism
32. Staff disciplinary and grievance procedures
33. Delegated authority and notifications to senior staff
34. Reviews
35. Dealing with aggression and violence
36. Risk taking

Appendix 1: Policy Issues for Inclusion in Staff Guidance

37. Dealing with sexuality and personal relationships
38. Working with parents/carers
39. First aid and administration and storage of medication
40. The complaints and representations procedures
41. Smoking policy
42. Alcohol policy
43. Drugs and misuse of substances policy
44. Gift giving and receiving
45. Whistle-blowing by staff

Appendix 2: Programmes of Training for Staff

1. Normal and abnormal child development
2. Basic residential child care skills and team working
3. Specific child care approaches and skills appropriate to the home's purpose and function
4. Exercising appropriate positive means of control over children in the interests of their own welfare and protection of others
5. Recording skills
6. Permitted and prohibited disciplinary measures
7. Use of restraint
8. Child protection
9. Issues of race, ethnicity, religion and culture
10. Dealing with sexuality
11. Health education relevant to growing children including diet and nutrition
12. The implications of HIV and AIDS when looking after children
13. Communicating with children, including those with disabilities
14. Health and safety at work, including food hygiene and safety with medicines

15. Fire precautions
16. First aid
17. The Children Act 1989, Human Rights Act 1998 and other relevant legislation
18. The provision of purposeful and enjoyable activities as part of a positive care experience
19. Staff supervision [for staff with supervisory responsibility]
20. Interview techniques [for staff with recruitment responsibilities]
21. Complaints and representations procedures
22. The requirements of National Minimum Standards
23. Specific child care approaches, knowledge and skills for their role in the home
24. Working with families
25. Undertaking risk assessments

Appendix 3: Source Documents

- Care Standards Act 2000
- Children Act 1989
- Children's Homes Regulations 2001
- Children Act (Miscellaneous Amendments) (England) Regulations 2002
- Health and Social Care (Community Health and Standards) Act 2003 (Commission for Healthcare Audit and Inspection and Commission for Social Care Inspection) (Transitional and Consequential Provisions) Order 2004
- Review of Children's Cases (Amendment No.2 and Transitional Arrangements) (England) Regulations 2004
- Advocacy Services and Representations Procedures (Children) (Amendment) Regulations 2004
- Children Act 1989 Representations Procedure (England) Regulations 2006
- Commission for Social Care Inspection (Fees and Frequency of Inspections) Regulations 2004
- Commission for Social Care Inspection (Fees and Frequency of Inspections) (Amendment) Regulations 2006
- National Minimum Standards

Appendix 4: CAE Publications

- Personal Guides:
  - Children Act 1989 in the Context of the Human Rights Act 1998
  - Children Act 2004
  - Child Protection
  - 'How Old Do I Have To Be... ?' (a simple guide to the rights and responsibilitiesof 0–21 year olds)
  - Residential Care of Children
  - Fostering
  - Crime and Disorder Act 1998
  - Sexual Offences Act 2003
  - Anti Social Behaviour
  - Domestic Violence
  - Childcare Act 2006
  - Safeguarding Vulnerable Groups Act 2006

Available from:103 Mayfield Road South Croydon, Surrey CR2 0BH tel: 020 8651 0554 fax: 020 8405 8483
e-mail: childact@dial.pipex.com

www.caeuk.org

Discounts for orders of 50 or more of any one title